Mokumé
Gane

IAN FERGUSON

A & C Black · London

First published in Great Britain 2002

A & C Black (Publishers) Ltd

37 Soho Square, London W1D 3QZ

www.acblack.com

ISBN 0 7136 6156 9

Front cover illustration: Bowl by Ian Ferguson,
photograph by Terence Bogue
Back cover illustrations: Jewellery by Steve Midgett
Frontispiece: *Ceremonial container* by Ian
Ferguson, photograph by Terence Bogue

Cover design by Dorothy Moir
Design by Keith & Clair Watson

Printed and bound in Singapore by Tien Wah Press

A&C black uses paper produced with elemental
chlorine-free pulp, harvested from managed
sustainable forests.

Note: jewellery making can sometimes involve the use
of sharp tools and dangerous substances. Please keep
items clearly labelled and out of the reach of children.
Neither the author nor publisher can accept any legal
liability for errors or ommissions.

CONTENTS

本目金

Mokumé gane in Japanese symbols, by Muneyuki Sawada

5

ACKNOWLEDGEMENTS

This book would not have come about without the foresight and assistance of the Royal College of Art and the University of Oxford, which allowed me to conduct the research described herein. RMIT University is thanked for employing me, which gave me the time and breathing space for writing this book, and for providing the necessary access to scanning and computer graphics facilities. The Science Museum Library is acknowledged for its assistance in researching the history of mokumé, as is the Victoria and Albert Museum for access to their collection. I have to thank Michael Rowe and Liz Olver for their encouragement and intermittent harassment (every time I went to London) as well as that of numerous friends and fellow craftspeople; 'When are we going to see the book?'. I am grateful to Mark Grimwade for his careful, erudite and precise editing of the metallurgy, and to Karl Millard for his often timely critiques (which caused me to re-write several chapters). And finally I have to thank the photographers of my work, Ian Haigh, Terence Bogue and especially Richard Muggleton for his immense patience, particularly in photographing the procedural images.

INTRODUCTION

'There was no special guild of goldsmiths or silversmiths: all art metal-workers were content to work in any metal, their sole desire being to produce objects which should be valued for their beauty alone. The value of the material was secondary; originality of design, grace in ornament, and skilful handicrafts were paramount; and so true is this that it is not in gold and silver that we find the most famous masterpieces, but in less costly metals and alloys.'

W. Gowland
Trans. and Proc. of The Japan Society, Vol. XIII, 1915.

I have now been a practising silversmith for 20 years and from the very beginning I was seduced by the whiteness and purity of silver, its malleability, its ductility, its forgiving nature, and it is probably (apart from gold) the cleanest metal to work with. However, perhaps because of its purity and whiteness, silver possesses some curious aesthetic properties. By itself, it can be remarkably bland, and despite (or because of) its brilliance in the polished state, it has the propensity to reflect its surroundings to such an extent as to almost disappear into them. This makes silver items highly reliant on strong, conspicuous form (and shine) to announce their presence. But when it is combined with other colours a remarkable thing happens; the silver not only appears brighter in itself, but it accentuates, enhances and brightens those other colours. From quite early on, I have searched for materials, patterns and colours to explore this dynamic between silver and colour. In early 1986 I found a metal technique that suited this quest.

Mokumé gane was developed solely for decorative use. A peculiar hybrid, it can hardly be called an alloy, because it is composed of several alloys, all discrete in their presence within the metal itself; a metal that has bemused and fascinated metal craftspeople since its invention. The technique has remained relatively rare and something of a curiosity, mainly because the traditional manufacturing technique is a laborious process and as many a craftsperson has found, a surprisingly difficult one to master. Bemusement generally appears when a craftsperson first attempts to make mokumé gane, usually with dubious to disastrous results. Not only is the manufacture of the raw material a complex process, but what to do with it and where and how to use it presents further challenges to the designer and artist. The fascination begins when a billet is successfully fabricated and the artist commences patterning the material; its chameleon-like quality, where the stroke of a file or a hammer blow can alter and shift a pattern, the seemingly endless variety and form the patterns can assume. The change of a patina can produce an entirely new range of colours, the intricacy and yet boldness of the surface which can seem to have a life and meaning of its own, often threatening to overwhelm the form and identity of an object.

Like many craft practices handed down through individual experience, the manufacture of mokumé gane has changed minimally over the centuries. And, like many craft practices handed down through individual experience, little has been written about the process and until recently that was mainly limited to articles in craft magazines and manuals on technique. I first came across mokumé gane when, as a student, I read about it in a manual called *Metalwork & Enamelling*, written by Herbert Maryon in 1912. In it he described a process for soldering the layers together. I tried to make a small piece of mokumé using the technique, and the results were, to put it mildly, unsuccessful. I had a mess of fractured, delaminating little pieces of metal of indeterminate, muddy patterns. I hid them in the bottom of a drawer and went looking for other ways of introducing colour and pattern into my work.

I realised that like many craft practices, the process for making mokumé is best taught by practical tuition; thereafter the practitioner must make, or repeat, his own mistakes. In 1986, I had the opportunity to attend one such practical tuition workshop, conducted by Eugene and Hiroko Sato Pijanowski at the Jewellers & Metalsmiths Group of Australia Conference in Perth, Western Australia. It was a very successful workshop, and all the participants walked away with approximately half a billet of copper/kuromi-do mokumé. On returning to my workshop in Melbourne Victoria, I attempted to repeat the process. Not having any kuromi-do, I decided to make a silver/copper billet; I took it out of the fire when I thought it was ready, gave it a couple of hammer blows and watched as this molten metal trickled off the anvil into a puddle on the floor. Although a disaster, it lit the fire of obsession which grips many a metal craftsperson: that of mastering and understanding a metal or technique.

So, bemused and fascinated, I began the long road in learning to control the traditional fusion process of mokumé. It turned out to be quite complicated, but each time it got easier and easier and there were fewer failures. Further improvements were made to the process and some experimentation was attempted; for example, I found I could increase the success rate by literally slamming the heated metals together with a powerful drop hammer. Eventually I created what I estimated at the time to be an entirely new combination of metals, a mokumé of nickel silver and Monel metal. I was looking for something that exactly expressed a feeling, and this metal mirrored that feeling (see frontispiece). However, the major problems still remained, namely that of knowing what exactly was happening, why sometimes it worked and sometimes it seemed as if the only reason it didn't work was because the moon was in the wrong quarter or there was no letter 'R' in the month. Why one combination was easy whereas another had a success rate dependent on the number of incantations and curses.

At the time I was teaching part-time at the Royal Melbourne Institute of Technology. In doing a bit of reading, I came across a process called solid state diffusion bonding, which shone a light on what had seemed an insoluble problem. This process showed me that theoretically there seemed to be a way of quantifying the bonding of mokumé; that equipment could be designed to control the bonding of mokumé, and it could be written down for repetition by others.

This book is a culmination of five years' research into understanding what happens when mokumé is fused together. It also contains all the other peripheral information gathered over the years as a practitioner: forging techniques, patterning techniques, patination techniques, the highways and byways of technique which make mokumé gane a metal of endless bemusement and fascination.

When writing a how-to book about a technique, it is always difficult to know how much information to put in, how much detail to leave out, whether the book is aimed at an audience of beginners or experienced practitioners. As this book is about new developments in a fairly complex technique, it is assumed that most readers will be familiar with standard metalwork studio practices and processes, so detailed descriptions on how to use a file, saw frame, repouseé punch, pitch bowl, milling machine, etc. are not included here. What is included are all the details directly connected to the manufacture and use of mokumé gane. Where other practitioners give relevant or more detailed information, these are referred to.

Disc Form IV, pendant by Steve Midgett. 18 layer mokumé with diamond and rubies in a fabricated sterling silver disc holder.

CHAPTER 1

Wood grain metal

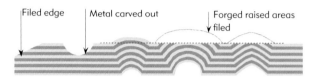

Section through Mokumé Gane showing layers.

Plan of Mokumé Gane showing pattern development.

Diagram showing patterning of mokumé gane

It is perhaps pertinent to formally introduce the material at this point. Mokumé gane was developed 300 years ago and literally translates from the Japanese as 'eye of the wood grain metal'. From its inception to the present day, the traditional manufacture of mokumé has used, both in pure form and as alloys thereof, the metals gold, silver and copper, with the combination of copper and shakudo predominating. The photograph overleaf shows Japanese tsuba using copper and shakudo. These and other suitable contemporary metals are described in Chapter 8.

As shown above, mokumé gane is made by fusing together multiple layers of alternating different metals. The metal sheets are initially relatively thick, so once the layers are bonded, the resultant billet has to be deformed considerably to produce a usable sheet of metal. The billet is forged and rolled out, reducing the thickness until the individual layers become very thin. Further forging, carving and removal of metal exposes the layers, which present a fine moiré or wood grain pattern.

Mokumé gane tsuba (sword guards). Japanese, from the 18th – 19th centuries. Courtesy the V&A Picture Library.

CHAPTER 2

Evolution of mokumé gane

Since their discovery by the human race, over the millennia metals have played a pivotal role in the evolution of societies, cultures and civilisations. Because of their importance in this evolution, those who were their masters and possessors have often imbued metals with a spiritual and temporal power. For example, gold because of its rarity and purity was imbued with the power of wealth, iron because of its strength, with the power of force; the possession of both implied political power as well. To reinforce this power, metals were said to be a gift of the gods, and in older civilisations, each metal had its own representative in the pantheon.

In their development and exploitation, metals have followed two distinctive but inextricably linked and intertwined paths: that of the utilitarian and that of the decorative. Even where the use of a metal has been of paramount importance, after it has been developed for its utilitarian purposes, humankind has always expressed its spiritual and temporal power through decorative, aesthetic embellishment. Indeed, the more useful or precious a metal was, the more attention was paid to its finish, decoration and artistry. Some metals have been used almost exclusively for their aesthetic value; gold having the most material value but of little use otherwise, was the obvious medium to express wealth, and social standing through artistry. Objects of bronze or iron on the other hand were primarily of a utilitarian nature, but even their form and usefulness were enhanced by decoration and those useful objects which belonged to the rich and powerful, were so embellished as to express not only their owners' power and status, but also the power and status of the object itself.

Nowhere was this decorative enhancement of the utilitarian using the artistry of the metalworker as an expression of power and status more apparent than in the culture of feudal Japan. Here, the Zen Buddhist and Shinto religions were based around the cult of the sword and the practise of martial arts, and use of the sword was accepted as a way of life and also the path to spiritual enlightenment. Swords themselves became the embodiment of gods and were revered. For this reason alone, there are Japanese swords over 1,200 years old, still in perfect condition, preserved in the shrines. This reverence led to considerable development in the manufacture of swords and the samurai sword came to be regarded as the pinnacle of the swordsmiths art. As the sword itself was held in such high regard, so owners wished to embellish the sword as a measure of their respect and the value that they placed on the blade, and synchronous with the evolution of the sword were the allied metalworking techniques. Although the Japanese did not embellish their swords as richly (i.e. with precious metals and stones) as was the fashion elsewhere in the world, they expressed the spiritual significance and importance of the sword through its fittings and raised their metal techniques to a highly developed art form, characterised by an astonishing complexity of metals, alloys, designs, colours and finishes.

By the end of the 17th century, the artistry of the Japanese metalworkers had reached new heights and the craft had attained an understanding of metals and created a range of decorative alloys surpassing anything produced elsewhere in the world. In addition, Japanese metalworkers had advanced their sword-making

techniques to a high level of skill, which, combined with extensive knowledge of metallurgy, freely exchanged information, the ready availability of the appropriate materials, and a large economy based on the metal trades, helped to make the invention of mokumé gane one of the more astonishing techniques developed by the Japanese craftsmen, possible.

The term *mokumé gane* comes from the traditional sword-making techniques, and it bears a superficial resemblance to one of the patterns that appear in the forged sword blades. Although a direct product of the swordsmiths' discipline, mokumé in its early form was obviously a cross disciplinary artistic inspiration, for the use of non-ferrous layered metals seems to have been a deliberate attempt to imitate in metal one of the *Tsui-Shu* techniques in lacquer work (*Urushi*) that originated in ancient China. This lacquer technique is referred to as *Guri*, where lacquer is laid in layers of alternating colours (often black and red), which are then deeply engraved to expose the different bands of colour. Indeed, mokumé gane was initially referred to as *guri bori*. The earliest attributed applications of non-ferrous layered metals on sword furniture are by Dembei Shoami (1651-1728), who is accredited with the development of the technique and the original name. He lived and worked in the Akita Prefecture; and was patronised by Sataki, the lord (or Daimyo) of Akita at that time. He was given permission to use the name Shoami by the Shoam School, which developed in Kyoto in the late 1500s and he is an historically important craftsman of the period who produced excellent examples of carved and inlaid steel sword furniture and fittings. Dembei Shoami was clearly influenced by sword-making techniques, and he found he could apply those principles to the forge welding of non-ferrous laminates to create mokumé gane. An early *tsuba* or sword guard attributed to him is made of alternating layers of fused copper and shakudo carved in deep spirals and patinated red and black, imitating *Guri;* an example of this technique is shown on page 12. He later referred to the technique as *mokumé-* or *itamé-gane,* a direct reference to the traditions of the swordsmith; a *kozuka* (small knife hilt) by him of gold, silver, copper and shakudo is made in the manner more commonly associated with what is now called mokumé gane.

The technique changed little in the ensuing two centuries, remaining with few exceptions a medium of the sword fitter, as in the *tsubas* shown on page 12. The metal continued to be employed in both forms, i.e. as mokumé-gane or guri-bori, and gradually developed into the patterned metal recognised today. However, it never gained widespread use. The demise of the sword-making industries in the late 19th century eliminated the traditional uses of much decorative metalwork, and an increasingly fragmented craft industry made wider use of mokumé in small items such as the clasps for *Fukurow-Mono* (document purses) shown on page 17. Much of this work was made for export to the West, such as the vase on page 16 and the drum-shaped box on page 18.

Mokumé gane vase (one of a pair), with gold inlayed shakudo, enamel. Japanese, 19th century. Courtesy the V&A Picture Library.

CHAPTER 3

Discovered & rediscovered

The opening of Japan's doors in 1854 after two centuries of isolation led to a fascination in the Western world, particularly Europe, with all things Japanese; not the least of them being the arts. The Reformation of 1868 and the edict of 1877 forbidding the carrying of swords were particularly fortuitous for Western collectors of the metal arts, as the newly defanchised samurai, reduced to penury, were obliged to sell their prized swords and possessions. Samurai swords and their fittings in their thousands left Japan until national concern halted the flow[1]. As previously noted, the metalcrafts were obliged to make work for the Western market in order to survive.

From the very first, although mokumé gane was highly prized by collectors as examples of the finest Japanese craftsmanship, it was also misunderstood as a material and a process. The earliest published reference in English to mokumé gane is made by Audsley in 1882[2] to 'the peculiar class of ornamental metalwork called by the Japanese

Clasps for *Fukurow-Mono* (document purses). Mokumé gane, various metal alloys. Japanese, 19th century. Courtesy the V&A Picture Library.

mokube (sic) in which a reddish copper is associated with syakfdo (sic) either in thin alternating lamina or in a fashion which produces a marbled effect'. In a misconception of the procedure he goes on to describe: 'In the production of this class of metalwork the several plates are soldered together then hammered'.

---

1 Joly, Red Cross catalogue, p. 95.
2 Audsley, *Ornamental Arts of Japan*, Section 6, p. 20.

Drum shaped box, bronze and silver with sides of mokumé gane. Japanese, 19th century. Courtesy the V&A Picture Library.

This misconception was reinforced with the published works of W.C. Roberts-Austen, one of the great pioneers of modern metallurgy. He was one of the first metallurgists to use the microscope to investigate the nature of metallic structures, and he was also instrumental in the development of the concept of phase diagrams, which are of paramount importance in this book in the understanding of what happens when mokumé is bonded. He also conducted pioneering work in the understanding of diffusion (see Chapter 6). He became famous for his scientific works and eventually was appointed Keeper of the Royal Mint, in which post he died. In his famous treatise on the manufacture of mokumé gane, published as part of the Cantor Lectures of 1888 and 1893[3], he described the technique and his experiments at soldering the layers together and even gave a recipe for the solder. This confusion was engraved in stone by the creation of the mayoral chain for the City of Preston by Sir Alfred Gilbert using the soldered mokumé gane process described by Roberts-Austen[4].

Roberts-Austen was instrumental in the acquisition of a pair of vases (see page 16) for the South Kensington Museum (now the Victoria & Albert). In his lecture he described the body of the vases as 'consisting of alternate layers of *shakudo* and red copper'. I have had the opportunity to examine the remaining vase and it is indeed made of these metals, but there is another metal there, which bears a strong resemblance to *shibuishi*. It may be apocryphal, but could Roberts-Austen in his early investigations into mokumé, have mistaken it for a solder?

World events then had an influence, in the form of two world wars and a depression. Communication, particularly

---

3 Roberts-Austen, W.C., Cantor Lectures, *Journal of the Society of Arts*, Vol. 36, 1888, pp 1137-1146 and Vol. 41, 1893, pp. 1007-1043

4 It is interesting to note that no one in Britain observed the similarity of mokumé gane to the already established techniques for manufacturing Sheffield Plate, not even Roberts-Austen. In his later lectures, Roberts-Austen was a little more circumspect in his description of the process as being soldered, at one stage in a lecture of 13/5/1890 (*Journal of the Society of Arts*, Vol. 36, 1889-90 p. 696) he stated that 'In their finest works, they apparently use no solder a (t) all, but simply trust to ordinary welding'. - !!

cultural communication, deteriorated and an even larger step backwards was made. The misconceptions of Audsley and Roberts-Austen were repeated through many metal craft manuals over the years[5] and the correct technique for making mokumé gane remained unknown in the Western world. The soldering technique repeatedly advocated in these early manuals is difficult to control and manipulate and has limited application. Until the 1970s the manufacture of mokumé remained a curiosity open to the experimentation of individual craft practitioners.

It was not until the early 1970s, when Eugene and Hiroko Pijanowski of the United States studied the traditional fusion technique of making mokumé in Japan under Gyokumei Shindo, Masahisha Yagihara and Norio Tamagawa, that the proper fusion technique became more widely known to western craftspeople. Through the 1970s and 1980s they disseminated their knowledge and experience through lectures and practical workshops to other metal craftspeople[6], which generated an explosion of artistic experimentation with mokumé.

Most of this experimentation occurred in the United States. However, the development of manufacturing has been largely confined to existing techniques; for example the development of the torque plate procedure (see Chapter 5 on contemporary techniques) produced a more reliable method of manufacturing the raw billet. In 1984 the company Shining Wave Metals started producing copper/silver and copper/brass mokumé gane on a commercial basis using the torque plate procedure.

5 Maryon, *Metalwork and Enamelling*; Wilson; *Silverwork and Jewellery*; Von Neumann, *The Design and Creation of Jewellery* & etc. The 1982 publication of Oppi Untracht's *Jewellery Concepts and Technology* was the first manual to include the traditional fusion process.
6 Pijanowski, *Goldsmiths Journal*, Vol. 3, No 4, pp. 20a-20h and Craft Horizons, Vol. 38, No. 1, pp. 32-35.

CHAPTER 4

Joining the layers – what happens

In order to understand what happens when two metals are joined together, it is first necessary to clarify some definitions and consider some aspects of atomic theory, which are applicable to the behaviour of metals. The second part of this chapter explains what happens at the metal interfaces when the atomic theory is put into practice to bond mokumé gane layers together using the following techniques:

(a)   Traditional fused mokumé gane, which can be either fusion bonding by sweating or solid state diffusion bonding or a combination thereof.

(b)   Solid-state diffusion bonded mokumé gane, which uses hot isostatic pressure bonding techniques.

Definitions

There is a considerable amount of confusion surrounding some definitions applied to metal bonding theories and techniques.

FUSION means the amalgamation or melting of different things into one. Fusion bonding or welding occurs when two metals are joined by melting them together, with or without the addition of more molten metal as filler. *Diffusion* takes place mainly within the molten metal. Fusion bonding includes: sweating, electric arc, resistance, plasma, laser and oxy-acetylene welding.

DIFFUSION means almost the opposite; spreading out, dispersing, de-concentrating and intermingling. Diffusion bonding or welding can be divided into two types: liquid state and solid state. Liquid state diffusion bonding occurs when a molten filler metal of lower melting point bonds to the surfaces of the solid parent metals. Due to its molten state, the metal is able to approach within interatomic distances of the parent metals and diffusion bond to them *without* melting them. Liquid-state diffusion bonding includes soldering, brazing and liquid phase diffusion welding. Solid-state diffusion bonding occurs when two metals are brought together and caused to bond by interatomic diffusion, without any melting of the metals. Solid-state diffusion bonding includes: hot isostatic pressure, friction, deformation, explosive and ultrasonic welding.

The atomic level

Bonding processes are complex and no single theory or mechanism is applicable to all situations, as bonding can be carried out over a wide range of conditions and with a wide range of metals. The most significant theories in the production of mokumé are interatomic metallic bonds and atomic diffusion. There are other theories such as ionic and covalent bonds and van der Waals forces, etc., which although important in the formation and attachment of oxides, intermetallics, and other chemical compounds, need not be expounded upon here.

INTERATOMIC METALLIC BONDS are non-directional bonds between atoms distributed at the points of a geometric lattice, that is the crystal lattice for the metal in question. Metal atoms consist of positive ion nuclei surrounded by electron shells, the outer shells of which form freely moving negative electron charge clouds (see drawing below). The crystalline geometry of the lattice is held together by the attraction between the positive ions and the free electrons. These freely moving electron clouds contribute to the heat and electrical conductivity of metals, and most metals can be deformed considerably because the atoms can slide past each other without completely disrupting the atomic bond.

ATOMIC DIFFUSION can be defined as the mechanism by which matter can be transported or dispersed through matter. Diffusion is a continuous occurrence in all substances, but the rates are dependent on many factors including relative atomic or molecular sizes, densities, physical state, crystal structures, etc. Diffusion in solid metals is restricted by the bonding of the atoms into a

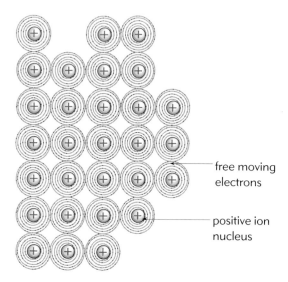

free moving electrons

positive ion nucleus

Interatomic metallic bond.

21

generally crystalline form, but it generally increases exponentially with increase in temperature until the metal is liquid, at which stage the crystal lattice breaks down, diffusion becomes very rapid and if two or more metals are present, alloying commences. The two main forms of diffusion in crystalline metal structures applicable to bonding processes are:

(1) Volume diffusion, which occurs within the structure of the metal.

(2) Surface diffusion.

There are two main mechanisms involved in volume diffusion – substitutional diffusion and interstitial diffusion.

When metals solidify, they do so in a generally progressive but uneven fashion, so the structure rarely forms a perfect crystal lattice. As some parts solidify faster, grains are formed and the orientation of their lattice can be in all directions. Substitutional diffusion occurs when there are vacancy defects in the crystal lattice and grain boundaries, and when there is sufficient energy, atoms may move from one position to another. As temperature increases providing more thermal energy, the lattice bond weakens, more vacancies occur and the rate of diffusion increases.

Atoms vary in size, as does the spacing in their individual lattice structures. Interstitial diffusion occurs when atoms move among the interstices of a crystal lattice structure without permanently displacing the atoms in the lattice. The relative differential atomic size of the diffusing matter to the lattice atoms must be sufficient to allow movement through the lattice. As with substitutional diffusion, an increase in temperature loosens the lattice structure of the metal, with a consequent increase in interstitial diffusion.

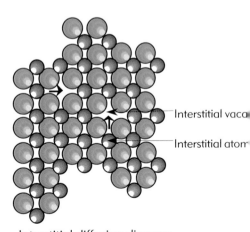

vacancy

substitutional atoms

Substitutional diffusion diagram.

Interstitial vaca

Interstitial atom

Interstitial diffusion diagram.

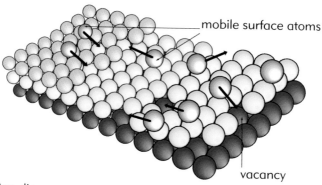

mobile surface atoms

vacancy

Surface diffusion diagram.

Surface diffusion may be defined as the continual movement of atoms from one site to another across the surface of a substance. Surface diffusion is largely thermally activated and the activation energy required is much lower than that for volume diffusion, the rate of diffusion increasing with temperature to the point where atoms commence to make jumps much longer than interatomic distances. Also because of this much lower energy requirement, the surface of a metal sheet will become molten before the interior; this is particularly important in the bonding of mokumé, as can be seen in Chapter 13.

To sum up, diffusion in a metal is continuous and increases rapidly with rise in temperature. Temperature also weakens the crystal structure to the point where it breaks down; the metal fuses and becomes a liquid. In the liquid state, diffusion is much higher and the freely moving atoms can more easily reach interatomic distances for bonding to other metal atoms and surfaces.

Joining The Layers

For two (or more) atoms to form a metallic bond, it is necessary for the interatomic distance to be close enough so that the cohesive forces can take effect. This distance varies from element to element, depending on the size of the atom but is generally less than 5 Ångstrom units – a very short distance indeed; an Ångstrom is one-ten-millionth of a millimetre. The drawing on page 24, for example, shows that copper reaches maximum attraction at 3.5Å, falling rapidly to 10% thereof at 10Å.

Theoretically, assuming *perfectly* flat surfaces and no intervening contaminants (i.e. the metals are prepared in a vacuum), two metal surfaces when brought together would form a metallic bond. However, atomically flat surfaces are a practicable impossibility and in

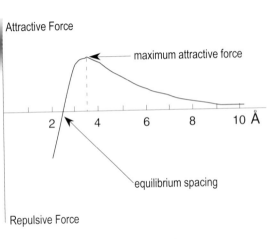

Attractive Force

maximum attractive force

2   4   6   8   10 Å

equilibrium spacing

Repulsive Force

Attraction and repulsion between
copper atoms.

reality most surfaces are full of holes,
ridges, steps and scratches and
contact can only be made over very
small areas such as the surface of
spheres or what are referred to as
asperities (microscopic ridges) on a
surface. In order to get the metal
interfaces within metallic bonding
distances, two stratagems are
employed: the cleaning procedure,
and the application of temperature
and pressure. As noted above, atomic
movements are very temperature
dependent and interatomic jumps
and diffusion increases rapidly, to
the point where the metals become
liquid and flow. Temperature is
therefore the most important factor
in the bonding of mokumé layers and
is used in every process. Pressure is
used to obtain close contact at those
asperities in the initial phase of
bonding, and as will be shown, is an
important factor in solid state
diffusion bonding.

Traditional fusion bonded mokumé gane

The traditional methods of making
mokumé gane and Sheffield Plate
employ fusion by sweating, where
the metals are heated until the
interfaces become molten, usually by
forming a eutectic. The classic
example of this phenomenon is in
joining silver and copper. The metals
melt at 960°C (1760°F) and 1083°C
(1982°F) respectively, however silver
and copper have a eutectic/solidus
line of 778°C (1432°F) over a wide
alloy range (see drawing page 97).
Woe betides any maker who, during
the fusion process, keeps the metal
billet above that temperature for
more than a few seconds!

(1)   Metal sheets are cleaned, the
surface being roughened to create
fine asperities (see Chapter 9). The
sheets are bound or clamped
together and heated in a reducing
atmosphere. Initially, the clamping
keeps the asperities or ridges on the
surfaces in close proximity.
Temperature causes interatomic
jumps to be made at these points,
forming metallic bonds, and this is
actually the first stage of solid-state
diffusion bonding. However, in the
traditional process, there is no
horizontal restriction, and as the
metal increases in temperature, the
sheets soften and are free to deform

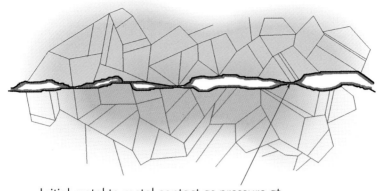

Initial metal to metal contact as pressure at asperities breaks up surface film

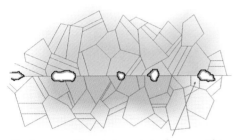

Surface melting brings interfaces within atomic distance and fusion occurs, agglomerating contaminants

Agglomeration of impurities and pore elimination

Disappearance of original interface and formation of new alloy, sometimes eutectic

sideways. The clamping system, being rigid, allows the applied pressure to dissipate.

(2) Increase in temperature eventually causes massive surface diffusion, with the surface of the layers becoming semi-liquid or melting, fusing the layers together. The liquid layer absorbs or agglomerates contaminants.

(3) The joint solidifies, often creating through diffusion another alloy at the interface – this can be seen in the drawing above, bottom right. In instances where no melting has occurred, solid state diffusion bonding takes place, activated mainly by temperature and time.

25

Solid-state diffusion bonding

Modern solid-state bonding techniques are basically an extension of traditional metal joining techniques, with the addition of scientific knowledge and precision. There are several significant factors of modern solid-state diffusion bonding techniques that have application to the manufacture of mokumé gane. The process can be quantified and repeated and quality control maintained. Production runs of many thousands, for example the manufacture of turbine blades and copper bottomed stainless steel saucepans are common. Multiple and complex welds can be performed in one operation; for example the wing boxes of FIll swing-wing bombers contain 66 titanium parts, which are all welded together in one operation. A wide range of dissimilar materials can be bonded, e.g. the synthetic ruby lens of a laser is diffusion bonded to the metal mirror. Although diffusion bonding has been used principally to bond titanium, superalloys etc., the process has been used to bond a wide variety of other materials.

The general process of solid-state diffusion bonding can be defined as occurring in four stages.

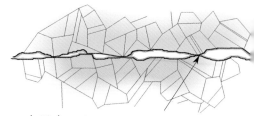

Initial contact as pressure at asperities breaks up surface film

(1)   Metal sheets are cleaned, the surface being roughened to create fine asperities (see Chapter 9). The sheets are placed in the control jig and heated in a controlled atmosphere. Initial pressure causes deformation of asperities and fracture of any hard oxide surface layer, exposing clean metal and bringing surface atoms within atomic distances at the interface.

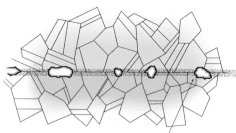

Surface melting brings interfaces within atomic distance and fusion occurs, agglomerating contaminants

(2)   Surface diffusion, accelerated by temperature creates initial bonding at asperities. Continually applied pressure ensures that the remaining un-bonded areas are progressively

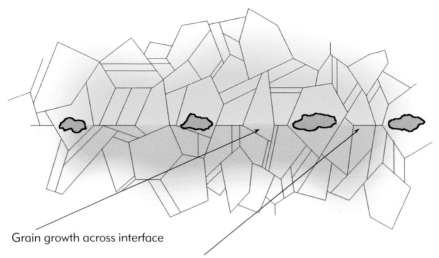

Grain growth across interface

Disruption of interface and surface films

brought within atomic distance and through surface diffusion; interfaces grow together rapidly, creating new grain boundaries.

(3)   The passage of time with the continued application of heat and pressure causes volume and surface diffusion, resulting in re-crystallisation and grain growth across the interface and the formation of a new grain structure (see micrograph of Copper-Gilding metal system, on page 94).

(4)   Dependant on solubility, volume diffusion causes interface contaminants to be dissolved or to form agglomerates in the parent metal. In the case where the metals are mutually or partially insoluble, the interface will form a grain boundary, as in the micrograph of the Silver-Monel metal system, see page 94.

original interface remains where metals are insoluble

Agglomeration of impurities and pore elimination

Disappearance of original interface

Traditional fusing.

CHAPTER 5

Contemporary mokumé gane

Currently there are two methods of manufacturing mokumé used by contemporary craftspeople: soldered and traditional fusion bonded. The soldered process is only briefly mentioned here, as it is a procedure unrelated to the subject of this book, namely diffusion bonding. Modern developments of the traditional fusion process are described to provide a comparison to the solid-state diffusion process. For more detail, various contemporary techniques are covered in other publications, for example in various issues of the magazine *Metalsmith*, journal of the Society of North American Goldsmiths, and notably in *Mokumé Gane; A Comprehensive Study*, by Steve Midgett.

Soldered mokumé gane

As previously noted, the process of soldering the metal layers together

was the result of an initial misinterpretation. Since the first description of this procedure by W.C. Roberts-Austen in the 1880s, many craftspeople have tried to master the soldering of mokumé gane; however the difficulties associated with it have meant that there are few who have made a success of the process. Among these are Eugene Pijanowski[1], who in his initial research into mokumé gane in 1968, described in detail his improvements to the procedure; and more recently, Alistair McCallum[2], whose individually developed soldering procedure has allowed him to create large sheets of the metal. All soldered mokumé gane has been made using the traditional metals of silver and copper and their alloys, and modern alloys such as the coloured golds, nickel silver, gilding metal, etc.

1 A comprehensive description of Eugene Pijanowski's soldering procedure is given in both of Oppi Untracht's books *Metal Techniques for Craftsmen*, pp. 182-4 and *Jewelry Concepts and Technology*, pp. 372-5
2 Alistair McCallum's soldering procedure is described in Steve Midgett's *Mokume Gane; A Comprehensive Study.*

Traditional fusion-bonded mokumé gane

Until the early 1970s, the traditional fusion process for manufacturing mokumé gane was virtually unknown in the West; it is mainly due to the efforts of Eugene and Hiroko Sato Pijanowski that the process was made available to Western craftspeople. The first process described by them, which involved wiring the billet together, (see photograph, right) appeared in 1978[3], and is a description of the method originally used by Norio Tamagawa in Japan. The metals, silver and copper and their alloys have always been used in this traditional fusion process.

In the late 1970s, the torque plate system was developed at the University of Southern Illinois (see photograph, page 31 and drawing, page 32). This was a major improvement on the earlier process in that the metal sheets can be more positively located and the applied pressure forces the sheets flat, ensuring intimate and uniform initial contact over the whole surface. This led to further developments in the use of modern alloys such as the

coloured gold alloys[4], nickel silver, gilding metal, brass and tin bronzes[5].

The metal layers can be round but are usually square for ease of cutting (see Chapter 9). The size of the

Wired mokumé stack ready for traditional firing.

sheets is restricted by the torque plates (which can get very heavy) and is usually in the range of 50-100mm (2-4in.) square – smaller plates are used for gold alloys. The thickness can vary from 1-4mm (18-6gge) and all sheets in the billet should be of the same size and thickness[6], although a thicker base sheet can be used to provide bulk and a plain surface on one side. The minimum number of layers recommended is 8; the maximum number is limited by the enthusiasm for cleaning! However, the height of

---

3 *Craft Horizons*, Sept. 1978, pp. 32-6.
4 There have been several craftspeople using gold alloy mokumé. For bonding, refer Steven Kretchmer; Aurum, English Ed., No. 25, Spring 1986, pp. 25-33, and Steve Midgett's book *Mokumé Gane: A Comprehensive Study*.
5 Mark Morgan produced mokumé using bronzes ranging from 5 - 20% tin content. *Metalsmith*, Spring 1983, pp. 37, 38

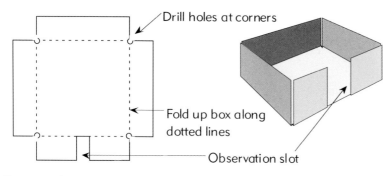

Drill holes at corners

Fold up box along dotted lines

Observation slot

Retention box.

Torque plate jig assembly.

the billet should not be more than $\frac{2}{3} - \frac{3}{4}$ the width of the sheets.

The sheets are annealed and flattened with a soft mallet; all surface marks must be removed and the sheets cleaned (see Chapter 9).

A retention box is prepared to contain the sheets (see drawing above) out of 0.6-0.8mm (22-20gge) steel sheet. The box should contain the sheets as closely as possible and should extend *almost* to the top of the metal stack – the thickness of one layer short (add the number of layers together). The gap in the middle is necessary for observation. All surfaces in contact with the billet must be painted with yellow or red ochre as an anti-seize compound, to prevent the metals from bonding to the box or plates.

The drawing overleaf shows a layout for the torque jig (the billet does not have to be on the diagonal – it can be square). It is constructed of two 6 – 10mm thick ($\frac{1}{4}$-$\frac{3}{8}$in.) mild steel plates bolted together with four

to eight 10 – 12mm ($\frac{3}{8}$-$\frac{1}{2}$in.) hex – head bolts. Weld on handles as shown; this makes it simpler to turn the jig in the furnace, and to hold it while removing the billet. Make sure the holes in the plates are slightly oversize to prevent the bolts sticking to the plates. Also make sure the bolts are as close to the billet as possible to reduce flexing of the plates. The bolts can be standard black or galvanised mild steel or stainless steel (which last longer). It is recommended before use that the nuts and bolts be heated to red to

6 The author has had success with alternating layers where one is half the thickness of the other, but the billet must be homogenous (the same all the way through) and balanced, i.e. an odd number of sheets, with the same on both sides.

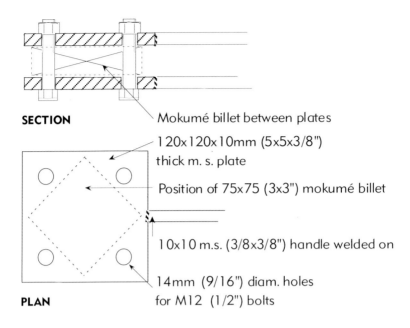

SECTION

Mokumé billet between plates

120x120x10mm (5x5x3/8")
thick m. s. plate

Position of 75x75 (3x3") mokumé billet

10x10 m.s. (3/8x3/8") handle welded on

14mm (9/16") diam. holes
for M12 (1/2") bolts

PLAN

Torque plate jig drawing.

blacken them; this helps to prevent
the threads from binding.

Put one torque plate on a flat
surface with the bolts in the holes,
pointing upwards. The sheets are
then stacked in sequence in the
retainer box, always handling from
the edges; do not touch the surfaces
to be joined. The lower melting
point metals must separate higher
melting point metals, and it is not
recommended that brass be in direct
contact with silver (they can rapidly
alloy to form silver solder!). Place the
retainer box in the centre of the
torque plate and put the top torque
plate over the bolts and do up the
nuts *without* moving the torque
plates or dislocating sheets. Using
two spanners, tension up the whole

assembly evenly by progressively
tightening opposite bolts, moving in
a circular direction. Another way is
to put the whole assembly in a vice
and tighten it up. Tighten the bolts
and re-tighten the vice, and so on.
Remember, the tighter the bolts, the
better the surface contact – a torque
wrench is useful, but not obligatory.
The whole assembly is now ready for
firing.

Firing in the blacksmiths forge

The forge is the most direct (and
probably the fastest) way of fusing a
mokumé billet; the whole process
can be observed from the condition

of the atmosphere to the actual joining of the metals. The forge may be gas or coke fired – page 28 shows a traditional firing in a gas-fired chamber. However temperatures can only be monitored visually, the judgement of which can require a considerable amount of practice.

The forge should be properly extracted to remove smoke, fumes and gases – particularly carbon monoxide, which is present during the firing. It is a good idea if the forge is in an area that can be semi-darkened, so the temperature of the billet can be observed clearly. To provide an even heat chamber, a 3-sided box is built out of firebricks over the fire. The chamber should be just high enough to be able to turn the billet over occasionally. Provide a lid of steel chequerplate or a firebrick tile and allow a slight gap at the back as a flue for the escape of smoke and fumes. Start the fire in the usual way; when the fire is well established and all fumes and smoke have cleared away, add either wood charcoal, coke or good quality coal (anthracite) and adjust the fire until the entire chamber is glowing red and full of blue flame. This means that the fuel is being incompletely consumed, but is using up all the available oxygen and the atmosphere in the furnace is inert – mostly nitrogen, carbon monoxide and carbon dioxide. Make sure the fire is even and there are no 'hot spots'. With a gas-fired furnace, preheat it for about half an hour beforehand to get the chamber to an even high temperature (red-orange), which can be maintained using a fuel-rich flame to consume all the oxygen.

Place the assembled billet in the fire with the observation slot to the front, bed down slightly and watch. With the wire tied billet, it can be started upside-down to heat the top plate initially, but it must be turned early in the process and fired upright so the steel plate can act as a weight. The torque plate assembly should be turned occasionally to heat evenly. **On no account must the billet be removed from the fire before it is fused.** When the billet starts to approach red to red-orange heat, observe closely. The billet will seem to darken momentarily and then start to brighten again; this is the

Upsetting billet after bonding.

fusion reaction commencing. As soon as it starts to brighten, quickly drag a steel pick across one of the laminate joints; if it shows a bright, sweaty line, remove the billet immediately. When fusing a billet containing silver, watch the silver only. Again, when the billet darkens momentarily or the silver shows a bright, sweaty surface, remove immediately.

On removing the billet from the fire, place on an anvil and tap gently with a hammer and steel block to drive the sheets together as shown on page 33. Place the torque assembly on the anvil with the bolt heads downward; place a steel block between the nuts (a scrap of die-stock is ideal) and hammer gently. Alternatively, quickly place the whole assembly in a vice or press (avoiding the bolts) and tighten; this process applies pressure more evenly. Using two spanners, undo one or two bolts and slide out the billet. Forge around the edges while still red to ensure that the billet is fused; billets containing silver must be allowed to cool to black heat before forging.

Note: if on removal from the fire, the billet does not appear to be fully joined, it can be returned to the fire in an attempt to fuse it more fully. However failure is a high possibility as once it is out of the inert atmosphere, the interfaces can oxidise quickly.

Firing in the kiln

Considerable success has been achieved combining the torque plate method with kiln firing. Using a kiln has obvious advantages: it is a cleaner environment and the temperature can be more precisely controlled. The disadvantage is that it is often difficult or impossible to make visual observation.

Preparation and assembly of the torque jig is as previously described; obviously the torque plates do not require handles. To control oxidation, the exposed edges of the billet layers are painted with hide glue or some other oxidising substance. The kiln is pre-heated to the required temperature[7] and the assembly is inserted for the required soak time.

Another method of controlling oxidation, developed by James Binnion[8], is to wrap the whole assembly in stainless steel heat treatment foil, packing granulated charcoal into the package to absorb remaining oxygen.

The author used a high power electric kiln with a stainless steel muffle and non-recoverable nitrogen or argon atmosphere. The torque assembly had to be placed in the muffle at room temperature, which was closed and the atmosphere was introduced from firing up until the end of the soak period.

7 Ard et al. used as a general rule a temperature 90°C (200°F) below the temperature of the lowest melting metal.
8 Detailed description of his procedures are in Steve Midgett's book *Mokumé Gane; A Comprehensive Study* or can be accessed through jbin@well.com.

Other variations

Since its first description by the Pijanowskis, there have been many variations and developments to the traditional fusion process.

Steve Midgett has developed a successful miniature torque plate system for making 25 x 25mm (1 x 1in.) billets of precious metal mokumé. It uses two steel plates between which the layers are clamped with a G-clamp, all of which is installed in a furnace made of two firebricks and fired with torches from outside.

The author had moderate success at one stage using a modification of the wire tied system. The billet, usually 50 x 50mm (2 x 2in.) by 17-24 layers thick, was assembled and heated with a reducing gas torch in a small open-faced firebrick chamber installed next to a 200-ton-force drop hammer. When (just) under the estimated fusing temperature had been reached, the billet was placed immediately under the hammer and slammed together with considerable force. Although moderately successful, quick, and a great spectator sport, the failures were usually attributable to difficulty in limiting oxidation and controlling bonding temperatures. If the billet was too cool, it would simply fly apart; if too hot the extra energy of the hammer blow could turn lower melting point layers molten, resulting in a potentially dangerous spray of very hot metal and a block of copper (or whatever) literally soldered together!

Limitations

Important considerations in the traditional process are:

1. Pressure cannot be controlled in any way, even though high pressure may have been applied initially (through the torque plates); when heat is applied, the softer metals of the billet simply flow sideways, dissipating the pressure which means that higher temperatures have to be used. For example, in the process described by James Binnion, where he uses lower temperatures, the loss of pressure must be compensated for by very long diffusion times at temperature, with attendant oxidation hazards.

2. Metals elevated to a temperature approaching the liquid state are highly unstable; the billet has to be removed from the furnace at just the right moment; too soon and the billet may be imperfectly (or not at all) bonded, too late and metals may alloy.

3. Eutectic reactions at the interface can rapidly alter the bonding temperature necessary and lead to alloying of the billet as shown overleaf. This should be compared

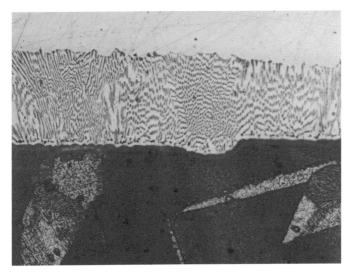

Micrograph of silver – copper eutectic joint.

with the silver/copper micrograph on page 94. Other alloys can form broad bands at the interface, which blur the definition between the layers and may cause undesirable low temperature working characteristics at a later stage.

4. Because of the reliance on high temperatures near the melting points of the metals, the conditions are different for each combination of metals and therefore practical experience is required for each situation. It is impossible to quantify the process and expertise can only be acquired through practical experience and judgement. The disparate bonding temperatures advocated by different practitioners are evidence of this reliance on individual experience[9].

5. Because of the reliance on high temperatures near the melting points of the metals, the lower melting point metals must separate higher melting point metals from each other. For example, if copper is next to *shakudo* and then silver, the copper will bond to the silver, but not the shakudo; the layers must be arranged thus: copper/ silver/*shakudo*/silver/copper/silver/*sha kudo*/silver, and low temperature phases can result when brass is used adjacent to silver.

In nearly all the above-mentioned processes, oxidation remains a problem, with consequent wastage of a considerable amount of metal from the edge.

9 For example Steve Midgett recommends 746°C (1375°F) for silver with brass and 778°C (1432°F) for silver with copper, shakudo and nickel silver, whereas James Binnion recommends 705°C (1300°F) and 738°C (1360°F) respectively.

CHAPTER 6

Solid-state diffusion bonding

This chapter will deal firstly with a brief history of the evolution of a natural phenomenon into what is known today as diffusion bonding. Subsequent to this will be the application of current scientific knowledge to establish the parameters for the solid-state diffusion bonding of mokumé gane, the design of the equipment and the practical application of the process.

Solid-phase welding has been in use by metalsmiths for thousands of years in the form of forge welding. Before the development of solder technology, early goldsmiths used hammer welding to join gold parts[1] and the forge welding of iron into larger billets is first found in the Early Iron Age[2]. The forge welding of iron and steel reached its apogee in the sword blades of Japan and the wrought iron manufacturing of the 19th century, before the introduction of Bessemer steel[3].

Scientific investigation into solid-state diffusion in metals can be said to have started in the 18th century when Desaguliers, a French scientist, friction welded lead spheres together at room temperature[4]. Interest in metals advanced with the Industrial Revolution and in the 19th century experiments were carried out in Germany, where freshly machined metal faces were bonded and heat treated to improve bonding; and by W.C. Roberts-Austen (yes, the same Roberts-Austen) in England who fused gold discs to lead cylinders at room temperature[5].

In the 20th century, the development of solid-state diffusion bonding has been dictated almost entirely by the aerospace and nuclear energy industries, which use high performance materials and the weld performance and quality control

1 Tylecote, *Solid Phase Welding of Metals*, p. 3.
2 Tylecote, *A History of Metallurgy*, p. 44.
3 Tylecote, *Solid Phase Welding of Metals*, p. 12.
4 Desaguliers, *Phil. Trans. Royal Society*, Vol. 33, p. 345.
5 Roberts-Austen, *Proc.of the Royal Society*, Vol.67, p.101 et seq. - he placed the gold discs on top of the lead in a cellar for two years, after which on examination they were found to be completely joined; he then left them for a further two years, after which it was found that the gold had penetrated 14.6mm into the lead.

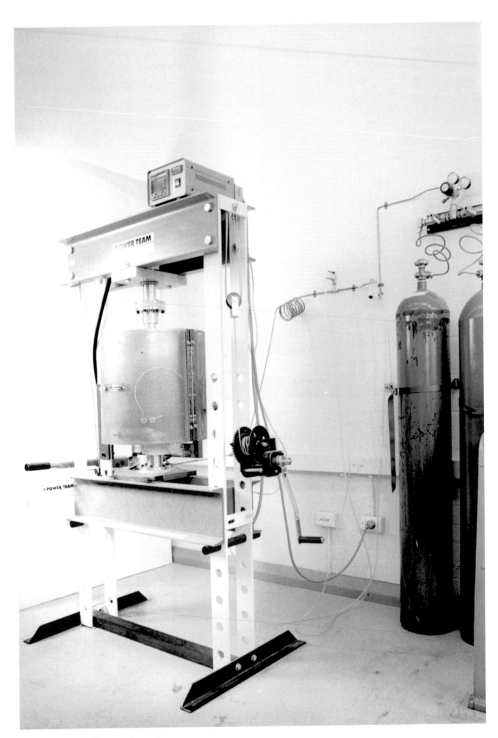

Solid state diffusion bonder.

thereof are of paramount importance. The exigencies of these industries have led to the development of a wide range of techniques and applications for solid-state diffusion bonding. These techniques include: hot isostatic pressure welding, friction welding, cold deformation welding, explosive welding, ultrasonic welding, etc. The technique that is used in the bonding of mokumé gane can be generally referred to as a Hot Isostatic Pressure System, or HIPS bonding.

Bonding parameters

As previously noted in Chapter 4, in order to achieve successful diffusion bonding of metals, it is necessary to control three major conditions, all of which are interdependent:
1. Pressure
2. Time
3. Temperature

An increase of one or two of these conditions causes a corresponding decrease in the required parameters of the others; for example the ancient practice of forge welding iron uses very high temperature, very high pressure in the form of hammer blows, and because these two parameters are high, almost instantaneous time[6].

Pressure An important variable; the significance of constantly applied pressure during the bonding process cannot be over emphasised. As previously noted in Chapter 5, lack of pressure control is the main limitation in the traditional process. Pressure is used to bring the atoms of each metal within interatomic distance sufficient to initiate bonding and the solid-state diffusion bonding process is influenced by the amount of deformation induced by pressure. When other variables are fixed, pressure invariably produces better joints[7]. Applied pressure is also important in reducing the diffusion rate between metals with disparate inter-diffusion rates[8], as excessive diffusion can often cause Kirkendall porosity or brittle intermetallics.

Time Is closely related to temperature in diffusion processes, however it is not a simply applied variable – this is described by Fick's Laws of Diffusion[9]. Too long a time at temperature can, through diffusion, promote the formation of intermetallic compounds, low melting point phases and increase re-crystallisation causing excessive grain growth[10], which can weaken

6   Ibid. Roberts-Austen used minimum weight and temperature, but a lot of time.
7   *AWS Welding Handbook,* 7th ed., p. 318.
8   Barnes and Masey, *Acta Metallurgica,* Vol. 6, January 1958, pp.1-7.
9   Ruoff, *Introduction to Materials Science,* p. 401. Wherein two substances will diffuse one into the other starting from zero time and diffusion; the amount of diffusion which is taking place decreasing parabolically with time to a level of equilibrium or stasis.
10   Schwartz, *Metal Joining Manual.* p.10-6.

not only the bond, but the metals themselves.

Temperature The temperature is by far the most important and the most controllable variable in solid-state diffusion bonding. An increase in temperature lowers the yield stress of the metals to be joined, allowing deformation to take place at lower pressures. As noted in Chapter 4, an increase in temperature also causes an exponential increase in diffusion rates, reducing the time parameter.

The reactions and behaviour of various metal combinations is discussed in Chapter 13. It is important that if you the craftsperson wish to bond a combination of metals other than those shown, then you must have a full understanding of the phase diagrams to which they are subject and to the bonding conditions and how they will behave after they are bonded.

The equipment

As any craftsperson knows, equipment comes in all shapes and sizes and qualities. Some equipment is more complicated because it does a more complex operation, and some equipment is more expensive than others because it does more, or it does it faster, or better. It is the same with diffusion bonders; most equipment for solid-state diffusion bonding is made for a specific purpose and it can be astonishingly complex and expensive. For example, the diffusion bonder at the University of Oxford used for the research in this book cost over £100,000 to build.

Fortunately, although it would be nice, this sort of machinery and expense is not necessary for a diffusion bonder used solely for the production of mokumé. However some expense is in order. A simple solid-state diffusion bonder specifically for making of mokumé gane, is shown in the drawings on pages 42 and 43. This diffusion bonder is composed of several discrete pieces of equipment and can be constructed as per the following instructions and drawings.

1. **A 25 ton hydraulic press**, the throat of which must be high enough and wide enough to accommodate and allow opening and swinging of the furnace (see page 42). Page 38 shows such a press.

2. **An electric powered clamshell furnace**. The chamber of the furnace should be just large enough to allow clearance for the muffle, thermocouples, etc. It should be of the light weight cast insulation type with embedded elements to prevent electrocution. It must be powerful enough to get to temperature as fast as possible; the furnace shown on page 38 is designed to 3.6 kW, and can use the domestic power supply. The furnace must be mounted on a

swinging arm to allow installation and removal from the press; the swinging arm can be fixed to the press or free standing (see overleaf).

3. **Controllers** – the furnace itself must be fitted with an override safety thermocouple with controller, and the bonding temperature must be controlled through a programmable control box with a thermocouple which is located in the base of the jig (see top diagram, page 43). The minimum furnace controls are; ramp rate, dwell temperature, dwell time and shut down.

4. **Extension rods**, which are attached to the press ram and table – the rods must be insulated from the press, as they get very hot. The rods must be made of a high strength, heat resistant super-alloy such as Nimonic 90. These rods can be clearly seen in the top photograph, page 44.

5. **A muffle** which fits closely around the extension rods. As it is not subject to heavy load, it can be made of stainless steel. The muffle must have a bleed valve and controlled atmospheric gas supply (see pages 43 and 44).

6. **Controlled atmosphere** – the gas supply, which is non-recoverable, must be controllable down to 1l/min. – page 38 shows a wall-mounted flow valve. Shown are two large bottles, one of nitrogen, which is suitable for all non-ferrous metals and is a lot cheaper than the other, which is Argon.

Argon is necessary for all ferrous metals, which react with nitrogen, and titanium, which reacts with almost every other gas as well. Fitted in to the supply line is a tap, with a tube line used for displacing air while loading the jigs (see photograph, page 45).

7. **Retaining Jigs**. These jigs are to contain the sheets of metal during the bonding process. The jigs must be constructed of a high strength, heat resistant super-alloy such as Nimonic 90. The metal is very tough and requires specialist machining – usually by those involved in the aerospace industries. This alloy retains its *full* strength up to 760°C (1400°F); and even though its strength tapers off rapidly above that temperature, the metal remains rigid and does not creep under load. The current design allows for up to two 50 x 50 x 35mm (2 x 2 x 1¼in.) thick large billets to be made at once (providing bonding parameters are compatible), or up to four 25 x 25 x 20mm (1 x 1 x ¾in.) thick small billets suitable for experiments or precious metals. The photograph top, page 44, is of the large jig currently in use. Larger billets can be made, but this necessitates scaling up not only the jig, but also other parts of the bonder, particularly the press. Various spacers may be needed to accommodate varying thicknesses of billet; these can be mild or stainless steel.

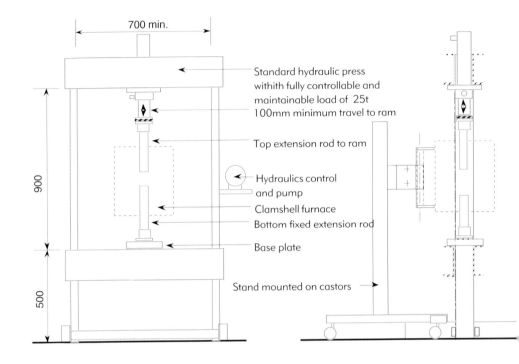

700 min.

900

500

Standard hydraulic press withith fully controllable and maintainable load of 25t 100mm minimum travel to ram

Top extension rod to ram

Hydraulics control and pump

Clamshell furnace

Bottom fixed extension rod

Base plate

Stand mounted on castors

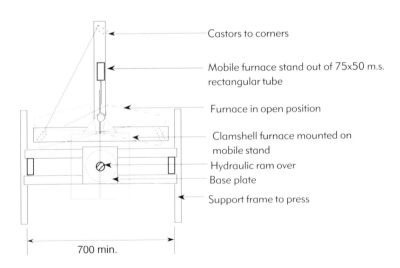

Castors to corners

Mobile furnace stand out of 75x50 m.s. rectangular tube

Furnace in open position

Clamshell furnace mounted on mobile stand

Hydraulic ram over

Base plate

Support frame to press

700 min.

Plan, elevation and section of diffusion bonder.

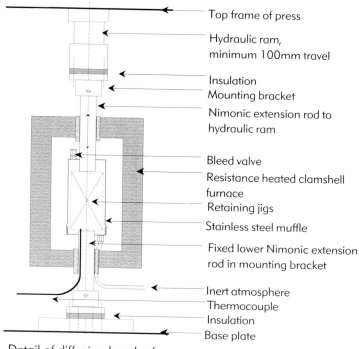

Top frame of press

Hydraulic ram,
minimum 100mm travel

Insulation
Mounting bracket
Nimonic extension rod to
hydraulic ram

Bleed valve
Resistance heated clamshell
furnace
Retaining jigs
Stainless steel muffle

Fixed lower Nimonic extension
rod in mounting bracket

Inert atmosphere
Thermocouple
Insulation
Base plate

Detail of diffusion bonder furnace.

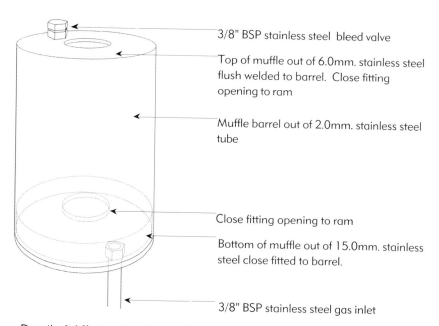

3/8" BSP stainless steel bleed valve

Top of muffle out of 6.0mm. stainless steel
flush welded to barrel. Close fitting
opening to ram

Muffle barrel out of 2.0mm. stainless steel
tube

Close fitting opening to ram

Bottom of muffle out of 15.0mm. stainless
steel close fitted to barrel.

3/8" BSP stainless steel gas inlet

Detail of diffusion bonder muffle.

Solid State diffusion bonder (furnace open).

The process

Once the basic process of solid-state diffusion bonding is understood and the required bonding parameters have been established, either from the tables listed (see Chapter 13), or the relevant phase diagrams, using the diffusion bonder is relatively simple. The metals to be bonded must be cut to fit the jig as described in Chapter 9 – there should be no more than 0.5mm play and sheets which stick must be trimmed to fit. The sheets are then cleaned, all as detailed in Chapter 9. Once cleaned, handling of metal sheets must be kept to a minimum and sheets should only be handled from the edges; if the surface is inadvertently touched, it must be re-cleaned using the described procedure. All metals, once cleaned, must be used within 24 hours.

In order to avoid unwanted bonding of jig parts and metal billets, the proper use of an anti-seize compound is critical, because if the metal surfaces are clean *anything* can bond together. A proprietary anti-seize compound such as Rocol 797 is recommended. Alternatively, white typing correction fluid may be also be used; this is basically Titanium Oxide in a solvent and it dries and sticks like paint. All surfaces not to be bonded must be

Disassembled retaining jig.

coated as shown above, such as the raised square and its edges in the bottom platen; the insides of the retaining platens; both sides and corners of the plugs; all spacers if used; if not, one face of one of the retaining platens; also the ends of the rams; the edges of the muffle.

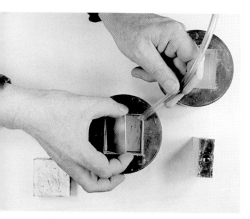

Loading the jig.

The jig can then be assembled; a retaining platen is placed on the bottom platen and the metal sheets stacked within, using an inert atmosphere discharge to displace air as shown in above. When the desired number of sheets has been stacked, a plug is placed in the top and the next retaining platen placed over it, using spacers as necessary so that the plug does not project too far into the platen. Repeat the stacking

if more billets are to be bonded.

Any number of layers may be used, but the retaining platen should be filled to no less than 2mm ($\frac{1}{16}$in.) from the top. Metals of differing thickness may be used in the same billet, however they should be evenly distributed to avoid deformation problems; do not intersperse a hard metal *occasionally* through a softer metal system, or place hard metal layers on the outer faces of a softer metal centre; these systems will be difficult to deform and tend to delaminate. A harder metal can be evenly layered alternately with a softer metal. A thicker plate to provide bulk may be used in the middle or on one side of the billet, however its mechanical working properties should be similar to the other layers in order to minimise delamination problems.

When the jig and metals have been assembled as shown below, they are

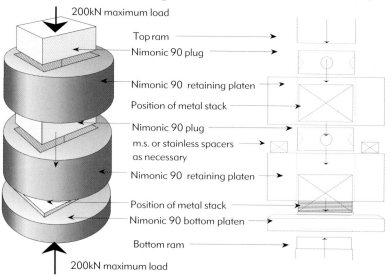

Stacking of retaining jigs.

Loading jig into diffusion bonder.

then placed in the diffusion bonder as shown above; the muffle is closed and the movable ram is pumped down to touch the top of the jig assembly. The bleed valve is opened and the muffle is scavenged for a couple of minutes with a high flow of atmosphere; the bleed valve is sealed and the gas flow reduced. The furnace is then closed around the muffle and the press is pumped up to the desired pressure. It has been generally found that a pressure of 32-48 kPa (2-3 tons/sq. in.) is adequate for the majority of cases. The furnace is started and the firing cycle commenced. During the firing, the bonder must be monitored to ensure the pressure in the hydraulic system remains constant (it may rise due to expansion); this of course can be overcome using a motorised, controllable hydraulic system, but that costs a lot of money. The atmosphere gas flow is maintained at 2-3 l/min. Once the furnace has attained dwell temperature, it may be reduced to 1 l/min. On completion of the firing cycle, the gas may be turned off, except in special circumstances (see specific metal combinations, Chapter 13).

The furnace must be allowed to cool to 500°C (930°F) maximum, at which point the hydraulic pressure can be released and the ram retracted. The furnace can then be switched off, opened and moved to one side to allow faster cooling of the jig, as shown right. When the assembly has cooled the muffle is opened, the contents removed and all controls shut down.

It may be found that jig parts have slightly stuck together. These can be separated with a wedge (such as a cold chisel) – usually a light tap is all that is necessary. The billet is removed from the retaining platen by placing the platen on two identical blocks; place a plug on the billet and hammer the billet out; the billet should fall out between the blocks. A light press can be used to push the billet evenly out of the platen.

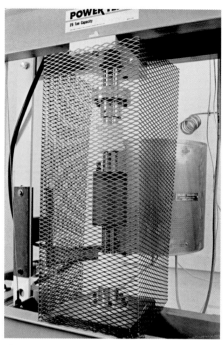

Cooling the jig assembly after firing.

In cases where there has been obvious bonding to the retaining platen (i.e. something went wrong – the metals have melted; pressures were too high; surfaces were not properly protected from bonding) and there is not sufficient force in the press to remove the billet, heat the whole to a dull red and try again. This may result in the delamination of the billet. Failing this, high hydraulic pressure may have to be used; avoid damage to the platen. If this fails then the billet will have to be carefully machined out, and next time you will have to be more careful.

Fine Silver/Copper/Gilding metal

Copper/Iron

Aluminium alloys

Copper/Brass

Copper/Iron

Brass/Iron

Copper/Titanium (etched)

Fine Silver/Shibiushi/Gilding metal

Fine Silver/Copper

Gold/Palladium

Copper/Titanium

Copper/Monel metal (etched)

Fine Silver/Nickel

Aluminium alloys

Copper/Stainless steel

CHAPTER 7

Metals

From its inception to the present day, the traditional manufacture of mokumé gane has used, both in pure form and as alloys thereof, the metals gold, silver and copper. By the end of the 16th century when mokumé was developed, the artistry of the Japanese metalworkers had created a range of decorative alloys using just these metals, with traces of metals such as lead, tin, and arsenic, which surpassed anything produced elsewhere in the world.

As previously noted in Chapter 3, mokumé remained something of a curiosity during the first 50-60 years of this century. With the burgeoning interest of Western craftspeople, who were not beholden to a traditional concept of mokumé, there was increasing experimentation with the many different metals available. The limitations of the traditional bonding process (see Chapter 5) restrict the range of suitable metals to copper alloys (brass, nickel silver, etc.) and the precious metals and their alloys including silver, carat golds, platinum and palladium. This range of metals is expanded considerably by using the solid-state diffusion bonding processes set out in Chapter 6. The metals suitable for mokumé can be divided into several categories: the pure metals and alloys, and ferrous and non-ferrous metals.

A vast range of metals and their alloys are available in sheet form through the modern metal industries, and for the production of mokumé it is simpler to buy from the manufacturer. The quality and alloy content are guaranteed, and as the material is usually produced in large quantities, it is actually more economical than making your own.

However, some alloys just aren't available, for example, any other colours of gold except yellow and white, and most of the Japanese alloys. It may also be desirable to experiment and make your own alloys. Although the composition of the metals is described in this chapter, the procedures for making some of the frequently used alloys are described in Chapter 8.

This chapter details the metals

that have so far been successfully used in the production of mokumé, both traditional and contemporary, including their composition and relevant physical data. The Metals Table at the end of this chapter lists the metals and gives pertinent thermodynamic and mechanical data. This list is by no means comprehensive, and there are many other metals that can undoubtedly be added to it in the future. A description of the combinations using the metals is presented in Chapter 13.

Metals

Gold Considered the noblest of metals, it is the only pure metal of a yellow colour. It does not oxidise, is very soft, and is the most malleable and ductile of all the metals, and heavy, with a specific gravity (S.G.) of 19.3. Gold has never been used in the pure state for the manufacture of mokumé, mainly because of its softness. Karat golds up to 920 Au (22k) have been used successfully, although these will oxidise when heated. It is recommended to use only 585 Au (14k) or higher, as the lower karat golds are not only insipid in colour, their hardness and brittleness makes them less amenable to the massive forging necessary. Karat golds come in several colours; yellow, rose, red, green, grey and white. All of the

colours apart from grey and white are really yellow gold with a tinge towards the other colour. White gold comes in several alloys: nickel white is the whitest, but is also the hardest; platinum white is greyer, but is more malleable and palladium white is greyer still.

Platinum The heaviest of the noble metals at 21.45 S.G., platinum is a hard but malleable and ductile metal. A pleasing silvery grey colour, it takes on a brilliant lustre when polished. It is completely inert and tarnish resistant. Most commercial grade platinum is sold as 950 Pt and contains 5% cobalt or copper.

Palladium Closely related and similar to platinum, sometimes the only difference appears to be the lighter specific gravity of 12.0 S.G., but it is slightly softer than platinum. Its colour is a darker and more neutral grey, it is also completely inert and tarnish resistant; however it readily absorbs large quantities of hydrogen at temperature. Also sold as 950 Pd, palladium can be obtained in a range of alloys down to 50%.

Silver The earliest of examples of mokumé using pure silver generally date from the 19th century. The whitest of all the metals, it has a S.G. of 11.4. Although very soft and ductile, silver does not diffuse into copper alloys like gold and its whiteness gives it a strong contrast with other metals. Pure silver oxidises minimally, but is susceptible to sulphur attack, which blackens the metal. Sterling silver (925 Ag) has the advantage of being somewhat harder, but due to the copper content, can present problems with oxidation and firestain. There is a new sterling silver called Bright Silver, which is firestain free that has been successfully tested for mokumé (see sliver/copper/gilding metal, page 48).

Copper Probably the most significant metal for the Japanese (and contemporary) decorative metalworker, the main attribute of copper is the myriad of alloys in which it is used. In its pure form, copper is unique not only for its pink colour, but its ability to accept a wide range of patinas. Copper tarnishes readily in air; this also makes it highly susceptible to oxidation and discoloration by numerous other chemicals. It is slightly harder than silver and lighter with a S.G. of 8.96, but is equally malleable and ductile. "Pure" copper comes in many grades, but the best for use in mokumé is called Oxygen Free Electrolytic Copper.

Shakudo The most widely used alloy in traditional mokumé, it is generally accepted as 4% to 5% gold in copper, although there are several grades down to as low as 0.5% and as high as 10%. Although it is commercially available in Japan, it

usually has to be made in the studio. The metal is pink with a purplish tinge in its natural state and can be patinated to a deep, lustrous purple/black, and is subject to the same atmospheric discolouration of copper. Increasing the percentage of gold gradually changes the patinated colour to a rich royal purple. Shakudo is somewhat stronger than copper, but remains extremely malleable. It can be hardened by adding 3% cobalt[1] without apparent deleterious effects on the patination.

Shibuishi meaning one-fourth, i.e. the alloy consists of one part silver to three parts copper, was the second most important alloy used in mokumé. It is not readily available, and usually has to be made in the studio. As with shakudo, there are several grades, traditionally ranging from 50% silver down to 13.5%[2]. Most of the shibuishi alloys are hard, springy and they work-harden rapidly, requiring frequent annealing. Their low solidus point of 778°C (1432°F) necessitates care when forging hot or soldering. The metal, depending on its composition, can be patinated a wide range of greys, brown grey and olive green, and is readily oxidised.

Kuromido Although considered a traditional alloy, it is a fairly recent development[3] of the 19th century,

---

1 This is a recipe that Steve Midgett uses in his book *Mokume Gané in the Small Shop*.

2 Gowland describes the traditional shibuishis. Ard et al. made several alloys down to 2% silver in copper, which gave an even greater range of patinations.

3 Although he does not name it as such, Gowland attributes the invention of kuromi-do to a Mr Y. Yoga, Superintendent of the Imperial Mint at that time, who added an iron-arsenic speiss to captured Chinese bronze guns, melted down for medals.

and is composed of 1% arsenic in copper. Like copper, it is subject to the same atmospheric discoloration. The metal is slightly darker and harder than copper, and can be treated in the same way. It patinates to a dark brownish black. As arsenic is highly poisonous, it is not recommended that this alloy be made in the studio. It can be obtained in sheet form in Japan.

Gilding Metal A member of the brass family, gilding metal is somewhat harder than copper and although very malleable, it work hardens to a tough metal. Golden pink in colour, it tarnishes readily like copper, but can be patinated quite different colours.

Brass There are many brass alloys; all are basically a mixture of copper and zinc. The most useful commercial materials for making mokumé are common brass (37Zn), and cartridge brass (30Zn), which is a deeper yellow and is more malleable than the former. Care must be taken when heating brass; the zinc in brass volatises at 900°C (1650°F), but can commence evaporating out at temperatures as low as 200-300°C (390-570°F), and prolonged heating can make the metal 'short', i.e. brittle. It can be patinated many colours and like copper, it is subject to the same atmospheric discoloration.

Nickel Silver Basically a brass with the addition of nickel, it is commercially available in 2 grades; the 10% nickel silver has a faint yellowish cast to it, whereas the 18% nickel silver is a neutral to warm light grey. The 18% nickel silver is distinctly harder than the other. Overheating nickel silver has the same effect on the zinc content as in brass.

Bronze Like brass, bronze comes in a vast range of alloys, a large number of which are hard and brittle and suitable for casting only. Bronze is generally a mixture of copper and tin, but most modern bronzes have other additives as well. The most suitable bronze for mokumé is a straight tin bronze; attempts have been made to use aluminium and silicon bronzes, but with no success. Ranging in tin content from 5%-15% and colour from pink to pale yellow; the metal becomes increasingly hard and intractable with the increase in the tin content. It tarnishes readily like copper[4]. Difficult to obtain commercially, a tin bronze may have to be made in the studio.

Nickel Pure nickel, a magnetic metal somewhat harder than copper, is very malleable and ductile. It has a S.G. of 8.9. Light warm to neutral grey in colour, it does not tarnish, but can be coloured using some patinas. It reacts strongly with some gases at temperature, notably hydrogen and nitrogen; it must be bonded in an argon atmosphere or vacuum. Nickel is classed as a

---

4 Mark Morgan produced a wide range of tin bronze alloys in experiments with mokumé, and found that alloys above 15% tin could only be hot worked (Metalsmith, Vol. 3, Spring 1983 p. 37).

carcinogen and some people can develop an allergy to the metal, so it should be handled with care and used with discretion.

Monel Metal A nickel copper alloy of a similar hardness and high tensile strength to stainless steel, it is nonetheless ductile, but requires mechanical means to deform it. A mid to dark neutral grey, it is generally inert and does not tarnish; however it reacts to hydrogen and nitrogen like nickel. Heating it to orange heat produces a tough black patina.

Iron The pure metal is almost as twice as hard as copper, but is very ductile and malleable. It has a S.G. of 7.87. Of light to mid grey with a bluish cast, iron reacts strongly with the atmosphere and will rust continuously if not patinated or coated with a sealant; it is one of the few metals where the oxide coating continually thickens. Like nickel, it reacts strongly with hydrogen and nitrogen at temperature. It forms strong electrolytic couples with other metals, particularly silver, copper and aluminium and their alloys.

Stainless Steel A ferrous alloy, it is nonetheless non-magnetic and corrosion resistant. It reacts strongly with hydrogen and nitrogen at temperature. There are many stainless steels; the most suitable for mokumé are the standard sheet alloys (304 and 316 series). It is very tough and cannot be deformed without the use of machinery such as power hammers and rollers. Of a light silvery grey colour, it can take a high polish and can be patinated several colours.

Titanium A refractory metal, titanium is noted for its lightness (S.G. 4.5) and strength – it is as strong as stainless steel, but more ductile. As such, it requires mechanical methods for its deformation. Contrary to popular belief, titanium is not inert, but forms a tough transparent oxide that protects the metal. In fact it is highly reactive at temperature and can absorb a large number of gases and react strongly with other metals, requiring specialised conditions for its use. Of a mid warm grey colour, titanium can be coloured by heating to a wide variety of iridescent rainbow hues known as interference colours.

Aluminium The lightest of all the polycrystalline metals in common use with a S.G. of 2.7. The metal is soft, ductile and malleable. A pale silvery grey colour, it forms a tenacious, but very brittle oxide which protects the metal. Due to its low melting point and ability to form low temperature phases, it is limited in its application with other metals. However, it can be combined with other aluminium alloys, which on anodising provide a differential colour.

METALS TABLE

Metal	Composition	Standard	Solidus/Liquidus °C	Solidus/Liquidus °F	Yield Strength Mpa	Tensile Strength Mpa
Gold	999/000 Au	999Au	1064.5	1948	0	103
Yellow Gold	92Au,4Ag,4Cu	918Au*	880/995	1615/1825		
Yellow Gold	75Au,14Ag,11Cu	750Au	780/910	1435/1670		
White Gold	75Au,.25Ni	750Au	955/980	1751/1796		
Grey Gold	75Au,25Pd	750Au	1395/1420	2543/2588		
Rose Gold	75Au,12.5Ag,12.5Cu	750Au*	780/930	1435/1705		
Red Gold	75Au,2.5Ag,22.5Cu	750Au*	900/910	1652/1670		
Green Gold	75Au,16.5Ag,8.5Cd†	750Au*	627/950	1160/1742		
Platinum	95Pt,5Co	950Pt	1750/1765	3182/3209		145
Palladium	99.5Pd	995Pd	1554	2830		145
Fine Silver	999/000 Ag	999Ag	961.9	1763	55	125
Sterling Silver	92.5Ag,7.5Cu	925Ag	830/895	1526/1640	72	255
Copper	99.8Cu	C101	1083	1982	69	216
Shakudo	92Cu,8Au	*	1055/1070	1930/1958		
Shakudo	95Cu,5Au	* ‡	1065/1075	1949/1967		
Shibuishi	50Cu,50Ag	*	779/875	1435/1605		
Shibuishi	60Cu,40Ag	*	779/915	1435/1679		
Shibuishi	67Cu,33Ag	*	779/940	1435/1724		
Shibuishi	75Cu,25Ag	* ‡	779/970	1435/1778		
Kuromido	99Cu, 1As	‡	1010/1070	1850/1958		
Gilding Metal	90Cu,10Zn	CZ101	1030/1045	1886/1912	69	255
Brass	70.0Cu,30.0Zn	CZ106	920/950	1688/1742	75	300
Brass	63.0Cu,37.0Zn	CZ108	902/930	1655/1706	97	315
Bronze	95Cu,5Sn	*	975/1060	1789/1940	130	325
Bronze	90Cu, 10Sn	*	850/1020	1562/1868	195	455
Nickel	99.98Ni	N1610$	1453	2648	59	317
Nickel Silver	62Cu,28Zn,10Ni	NS101	935/1020	1720/1870	125	340
Nickel Silver	62Cu,20Zn,18Ni	NS106	1060/1110	1940/2030	185	415
Monel Metal	63Ni,Cu,2.5Fe,2.0Mn	M400$	1300/1350	2372/2462	240	550
Stainless Steel	18.0Cr,8.0Ni	304S15	1415/1460	2579/2660	230	480
Iron	99.5Fe	FE410$	1535	2795	150	210
Titanium	99.6Ti	Grade 1.	1660	3020	255	370
Aluminium	99Al,1Mn	5005	632/652	1172/1208	41	125
Aluminium	Al,4.4Cu,1.5Mg,0.6Mn	2024	502/638	936/1178	345	485

* Studio manufactured alloy. † DANGER Cadmium vapour is poisonous! ‡ Available from Japan only

$ Available from scientific suppliers.

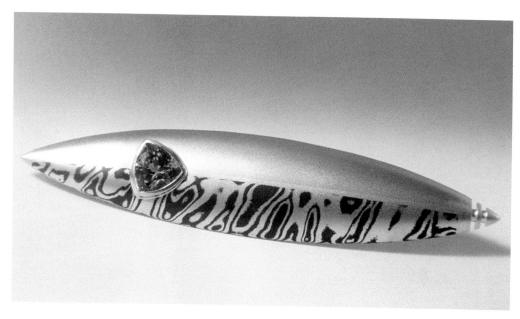

Shield form pin/pendant by Steve Midgett. Platinum and shakudo mokumé and 22k gold.

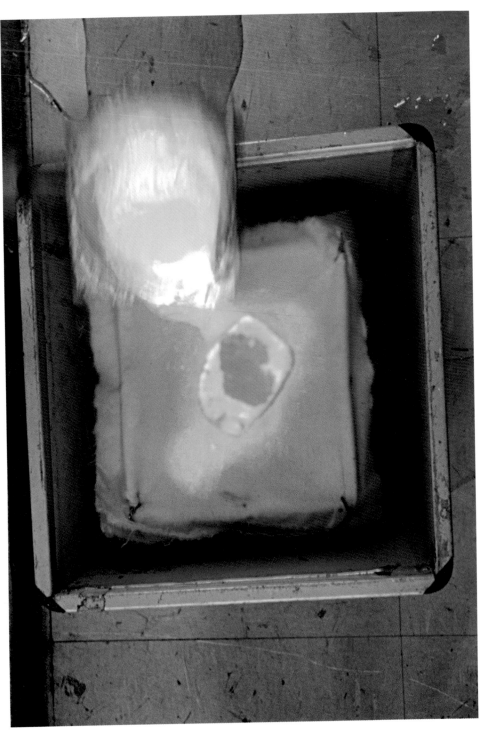

Casting ingot in Japanese water mould.

CHAPTER 8

Alloying, casting & rolling

The metals suitable for casting in the small studio are usually of the non-ferrous or precious metal series. Metals such as platinum, palladium (and their alloys), ferrous metals and the refractive metals require high temperature (and hi-tech) equipment. When alloying metals, use clean, pure metals wherever possible, when using alloy scraps, be absolutely sure of its composition. Use either granules or snip the metal into smallish pieces. The metal may be melted in an open ceramic crucible, a salamander or an induction electro-melt. Keep separate crucibles for each alloy (one for all the *shibuishi* alloys is sufficient). The ingot mould should be suitable for making sheet; a simple mold can be made of two mild steel sheets of minimum 6mm (¼in.) thickness, separated by a spacer made of square mild steel rod 3–6mm (⅛-¼in.), depending on the size of ingot required, bent in a 'U' shape and linished flat on both sides, all held together with a G-clamp – The photo above shows an ingot mould assembly with a cast ingot.

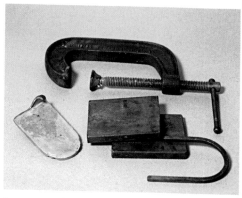

Ingot mould.

The mould should be warmed beforehand to approximately 150°C (300°F) to prevent short freezing and drive out any moisture. Blacken the inside with a little soot (acetylene soot is ideal) to absorb oxygen during the pour. Set the mould upright or at a slight incline to the vertical in a shallow tray to catch any spillage. Clean the tray after each different melt to prevent mix of spilled metals.

Put the metals in the crucible, sprinkle with a little borax and charcoal and melt higher melting point metals first, or in the case of predominately precious metals, the nobler. Add the other metals in descending order of melting point or nobility. When the melt develops a shimmery, liquid surface, stir with a graphite stick, return the flame to the top of the crucible and keeping there to prevent oxidation, pour the melt steadily and quickly into the mould.

When solidified, clean up the ingot, heat to a dull red and forge the faces and edges. This is important and has the effect of refining the grain, removing solidifying stresses and hammering out defects. Some metals cannot be forged at red heat, particularly silver/copper alloys and some bronzes and should be allowed to cool to black before forging.

Metals used by the traditional Japanese craftsmen were cast in ingot form in a unique way – under water. Silver, copper, *shakudo* and *shibuishi* are cast in this fashion[1]. Whether this process is of any great advantage over contemporary procedures of casting into a closed mould has never been sufficiently analysed, and traditional alloys have been successfully cast in steel moulds. However, it would appear that casting copper and its alloys under water goes some way to excluding gases from the ingot and provides a clean, dense surface.

A metal frame is prepared, over which is draped 2-5 layers of heavy cotton (**no** synthetics) duck or twill. This is dished to collect the metal and the cloth is wired or sewn to the metal frame – approximately 200 x 150mm (8 x 6in.) would be the maximum. Do not attempt to make the ingot thin and flat; this will cause porosity and trapped bubbles. The photo below shows an ingot mould capable of holding 400-450 g (12-14oz). Large ingots (i.e. over 500g) necessitate making the receptacle very sturdy and with many layers of cloth.

Thoroughly saturate the cloth and submerge the receptacle in a container full of hot water (80-90°C); the water should cover it to a depth of approximately 25-50mm (1-2in.), as shown on page 56. Make sure there are no trapped air bubbles under the cloth.

Melt the metals as described previously. When molten, pour the melt steadily and quickly into the receptacle, from a height of not more than 150mm above the surface of the water, as shown on page 56. The

Traditional Japanese ingot mould.

1 Gowland was probably the first to describe this process in the West. He maintained that the method of casting under water was to prevent surface oxidation of low grade silver, particularly coinage.

metal will sit very clearly in a molten state in the cloth for several seconds before solidifying, at which stage the water will bubble fiercely. When the bubbling has stopped, the ingot can be removed (it will still be **hot**), and should look bright and shiny. If the metal burns through the cloth and ends up as a mess in the bottom of the bath, then there was too much metal for the thickness of cloth present, or a trapped air bubble.

Examine the ingot and file out any bubbles or imperfections. Because the ingot will be an irregular, round cake-like shape due to the shape of the mould, it is necessary to forge it into a squared shape suitable for rolling as described above. Traditionally for *Shakudo* and *Shibuishi*, the ingot casting process was repeated twice more to ensure that the metals were properly mixed. However in the past, heat sources were not as efficient or of sufficiently high a temperature. Modern heat sources are much more powerful and if the melt is well molten and stirred, this procedure should be unnecessary[2].

Once the ingot has been cast and forged and is ready for rolling, clean it either by linishing the surface (make sure grit and other metal isn't ground into the surface) or by firstly annealing and pickling and then boiling in water for 20 minutes with a teaspoon of bicarbonate of soda per litre.

Make sure the rollers are spotless: wipe carefully and remove as much oil as possible. Firstly carefully roll the ingot to the **width** required, allowing for scrap at the edges. Anneal, forge down the leading edge to prevent splitting of the ingot through the middle and roll in one direction to the required thickness. Rolling to provide multiple widths, i.e. two or three sheet sizes wide, cuts down wastage. Here, power rollers are a great asset; if these are not available, depending on metal being rolled, it may be necessary to roll only one sheet wide. Roll the strips as long as possible; it makes it easier to straighten and flatten it **before** cutting it up into the required sheets. Also, getting someone to tension the sheet as it comes out is a great help in keeping it flat. Passing the metal through the rollers at the same setting several times can also assist in keeping sheets flat. After what is estimated to be the last anneal, pickle and clean again; carefully clean the rollers again and roll to thickness, keeping the sheet in its work-hardened state; the surfaces should then remain clean enough.

2 In their early work with shibuishi alloys, Ard et al. found it necessary to carry out the traditional 3-times-melt for alloys above 15% silver. The author has not had this problem.

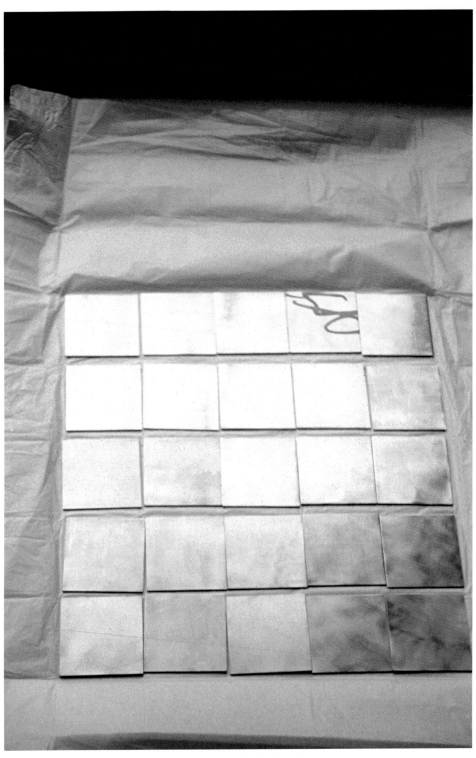

Brass/monel metal sheets cleaned and ready for bonding.

CHAPTER 9

Metal preparation

The preparation and cleaning of metals is at once the most tedious and laborious of the processes in making mokumé; and the most important. This is also the first critical stage in the journey towards a successful billet. Thorough and careful preparation of the metals to be used can save a lot of time, trouble and wastage. Practice makes perfect and all things being equal (i.e. the metals are relatively clean, flat and scratch free), it is possible to mark, cut up and check the fit of 30–35 sheets in one hour. It is also possible to clean 30–35 sheets ready for bonding in two hours. When I am really efficient and organised, I can prepare the metals for two 25-layer billets in a morning.

Cleanliness of the metal sheets is perhaps the most important stage in sheet preparation – all traces of dirt, contaminants, scales and oxides must be scrupulously removed from the metal faces to be bonded. Without the presence of surface films and contaminants there is no doubt that the bonding of Mokumé would be easier. However, absolute cleanliness of surface is difficult to achieve and maintain. As there is an attractive force between the metal atoms, so there are attractive forces between them and all other atoms and molecules such as air, water, gases and oils. Surface films can be divided into two groups, both of which may be present at the same time: oxide films, which are a chemical reaction between the metal and the atmosphere, and absorbed or adherent contaminants, both gaseous and liquid.

Although it is important to remove these contaminants, only the absorbed or adherent kind (such as dirt, oil, etc.) can be permanently removed. Oxide films are a significant factor, as a metal surface can never be said to be oxide free[1], and although the oxide film inhibits the bonding process, it does not prevent it happening (unless too

1 There has been much discussion amongst metallurgists for years as to whether the nobler metals (gold, platinum, palladium) actually oxidise at room temperature; the fact that oxides of these metals exist presents the possibility. Silver for example oxidises, but the coating is so thin as to be invisible.

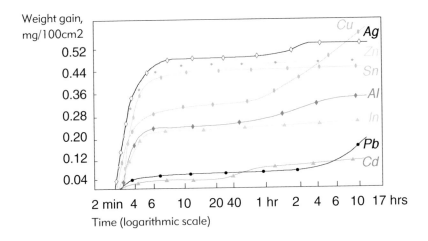

Oxidation of pure metals at room temperature.

thick, of course). The majority of metals react with atmospheric oxygen to form oxide coatings varying from 20–1000 Ångstroms thick. Films start forming immediately and continuously at room temperature; in fact, as the graph (above) shows, a lot of metals can gain up to 80% of their natural oxide coating within ten minutes[2]! And, as the graph shows, on some other metals such as copper, lead and iron, the oxide film just keeps on getting thicker with the passage of time.

Tools

Equipment can be as basic or complicated as desired. For marking out, a metal ruler, scribe and engineer's square are sufficient.

For cutting sheet up to 1.6mm (14gge) thick a small foot operated guillotine is necessary – I have found that this tool will cut all the metals used in mokumé. This includes titanium and stainless steel, so long as they are not too thick – 1mm. (18gge) is about the maximum. Do not use bench shears as they curve the sheet. For the hi-tech a suitable clipping die is a time and labour-saving (albeit expensive) device. For thicker metal a hacksaw is necessary and a bandsaw desirable. When sheet has to be manufactured in the studio (see Chapter 8), a good set of 100mm (4in.) minimum width geared flat rollers is necessary, and power rollers are a considerable advantage. For cleaning, 220–240 silicon carbide wet and dry paper, a sanding block and a means of securing the metal sheets is all that

2 Vaidyanath and Milner, to whom this graph is attributed, conducted tests on surface oxidation of metals in their research into the surfaces suitable for diffusion bonding.

is required (see page 65). I have also used one of those small orbital sanders with the triangular base that looks like an old clothes pressing iron. This is very efficient and saves a lot of muscle power, but the metal sheets must be *absolutely* flat and care must be taken not to round the edges.

Material preparation

As stated in Chapter 7, it is simpler to acquire metals from a commercial manufacturer; the standard is constant, the metal is of even thickness, clean, and the sheets are flat. As well, these days metal sheets are often supplied bright milled with a protective plastic film. If possible, always buy sheets in the work-hardened state – at least a quarter-hard. This is advantageous in handling. The sheets don't bend or acquire deep scratches and it restricts' 'rollover' at the edges when guillotining – the less rollover, the less wastage, particularly with soft metals such as copper and fine silver.

If, on the other hand, it has been necessary to make the metals in the studio, the finished sheets do not have to be perfectly flat; flatness is only important in making it easier to clean them. If there are unavoidable ripples from rolling, anneal and straighten the rolled strip as much

as possible, then cut it up to size and mallet the sheets as flat as possible on a flat plate with a soft leather mallet. Do this in a clean dust free area to avoid hammering bits of dirt into the sheets.

Cutting

Accurate cutting of sheets is necessary to prevent wastage; sheets that overlap others tend to fold under the firing conditions and unless trimmed, can lead to splitting during the forging process. Accurate sheet size is even more critical in the solid-state diffusion bonding process (see Chapter 6). Usually, square sheets are used because there is little or no wastage involved. However, for really accurate cutting, a disc-clipping die is ideal. This means of course that the billet will be round, and it also means that for the solid-state diffusion bonding process, the control jig must be cylindrical.

Most of the metal sheets described in this book are of a thickness in the 0.5-1.6mm (24-14gge) range, and can be cut by a guillotine. The best way to accurately mark out is to measure with a steel rule from one edge of the sheet and scribe at the end of the rule, moving the rule in multiples of the desired measurement. Firstly, strips of the required width are cut; these may curve and twist slightly if the strips are long. Manually straighten and take out the twist.

The strips are marked again and the individual sheets cut. In order to keep the sheets square, butt an engineer's square up against the lower blade of the guillotine, align the strip against it, hold, **REMOVE** the square – !!! – and cut. This way, square sheets can be cut quickly and accurately to 0.25mm ($^{10}/_{1000}$ in.) tolerance. Some guillotines have a squaring edge to one side; this is convenient, but continued use of the same position on the blade can blunt it.

Where the sheet of greater thickness – 2mm (12gge) or more – is used for bulk or as a plain sheet on one side, in order to minimise edge rollover it may be necessary to hacksaw or bandsaw the sheet and accurately linish or file to size.

When the required number of sheets has been cut, check for accuracy and reject those sheets more than a millimetre too small or re-cut (if too big). Where using solid-state diffusion bonding equipment, sheets must be within 0.25mm ($^{10}/_{1000}$ in.) tolerance: *it is necessary to test every sheet in the retaining jig to make sure it will fit!*

Cleaning

Through a long tradition, the Japanese craftsmen developed a process for cleaning the metal sheets that produced a surface still found to be the most suitable for bonding. The metal sheets were cleaned by boiling in lixiviated wood ash (basically a natural lye or alkaline solution)[3] and were then scrubbed all over with charcoal blocks, dipped in a plum vinegar and salt solution, washed again in a weak lye, rinsed in clean water and dried. More recently, there have evolved several recipes for cleaning[4]; nitric acid dipping; potassium cyanide dipping; boiling in a bicarbonate of soda solution and scrubbing with pumice and a scouring pad; rubbing with 320 grit silicon carbide paper pickling and degreasing with a hydrocarbon; scrubbing with dishwashing liquid and a glass brush and so on.

The procedures recommended here are those that have previously been used successfully by myself and others[5] and produce basically the same clean surfaces as the traditional Japanese method. The procedure does two things; it cleans the metal and most importantly it provides an ideal surface for bonding (see Chapter 4). Cleaning should be carried out in the cleanest conditions possible. Metal sheets with deep scratches or pits should be discarded: it is almost impossible

---

3 This cleaning process was used when all metals were made in the studio; it is not necessary when using modern manufactured metals.

4 Most of these procedures are described in more detail in Steve Midgett's book.

5 Vaidyanath and Milner. Their research found this to be the most reliable and consistent surface preparation for diffusion bonding.

to clean them and they can contain enough contaminants, which at temperature can diffuse through the whole joint, to cause delamination. At the very least, they may cause localised internal bubbling and delamination. Handling of metal sheets must be kept to a minimum and always from the edges; thoroughly wash your hands before starting. Some may wish to wear surgical rubber gloves for protection.

Silicon carbide 220-240 grit wet and dry paper is wrapped around a small, flat sided block of wood or metal – pick a size that is comfortable in the hand and doesn't waste too much paper. It is better if you can retain the metal sheet without touching it – a suitable retention jig is shown below, or simply hammer 4-8 small nails into a block of wood, driving in until the heads are just *below* the thickness of the sheets to be cleaned. Place the

cleaning jig on several layers of old newspaper as a soak. The metal face is then cleaned in a rotary sanding motion using liberal amounts of distilled water as shown overleaf. Avoid rounding the edges. Clean once, rotate 90° and repeat; do this twice more and the metal should be clean. Rotate the wet and dry paper as required; experience will dictate this – harder metals will wear out the paper faster. Paper that is too blunt uses up too much energy, doesn't clean properly and doesn't roughen the surface sufficiently. If the surfaces have curves or ripples, as happens with studio manufactured metals, be extra vigilant when cleaning in the concave areas and be careful not to abrade too heavily the convex areas and edges.

Turn and do the other side (it is not necessary to do both sides of the top and bottom layers).

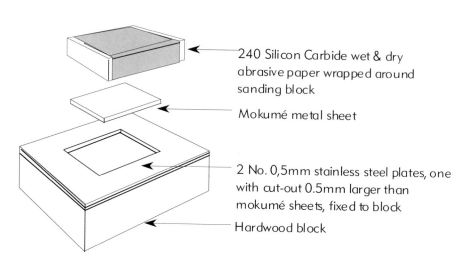

240 Silicon Carbide wet & dry abrasive paper wrapped around sanding block

Mokumé metal sheet

2 No. 0,5mm stainless steel plates, one with cut-out 0.5mm larger than mokumé sheets, fixed to block

Hardwood block

Cleaning jig.

Cleaning metal sheets.

The use of water in the cleaning process does several things: it suppresses metal dust; it acts as a barrier to the silicon carbide grit and prevents it from being ground into the metal surface; and it acts as a colloidal suspension medium and floats away all the oil, dirt, dust and oxide, off the metal and onto the newspaper.

Metals can be judged to be clean by:

(a)   Visual inspection – the metal should be bright and shining and completely free of any discoloration.

(b)   The water test – clean distilled water should cling to the surface as in photo, opposite, botom; 'balling' or 'peeling back' from the edges or surface indicates

contamination, usually grease or oil as can be seen opposite, top. When the metal sheet has been cleaned, rinse in distilled water and dry. Some people recommend using a blow dryer, but I find that this can encourage oxide build-up and also allows the re-deposition of any contaminants in the water. A cotton cloth is suitable for drying, but I have found there is available a wide range of industrial lint free, highly absorbent paper towels (which don't disintegrate). When dry, arrange the sheets in rows and wrap in acid free tissue (see page 60), keeping the surfaces separated by tissue, until ready for use. I save time by cleaning all the sheets of one metal in a combination all at once. Keep each cleaned sheet in a bath of distilled water until all are done, then dry and wrap them. Replace the water and do the next set.

All metals, once cleaned, must be used as soon as possible to mitigate any further contamination. As noted above, they will oxidise quite rapidly, which makes it impossible to bond an absolutely clean metal surface. I have found that the acid-free tissue protects them quite well, and I can store them for a maximum of 24 hours and still achieve successful bonding. Longer than that, the sheets should be re-cleaned.

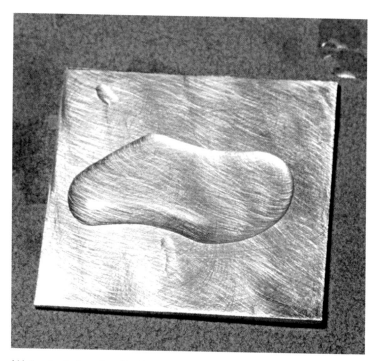

Water test showing 'balling' on contaminated metal.

Water test showing cleaned metal.

Rolling large sheets of mokumé gane.

CHAPTER 10

Forging & rolling the billet

Once the billet of mokumé gane has been bonded, it is then necessary to deform it to the desired shape. Initially the billet is forged to consolidate the bonds and reduce it to fit the rollers, or it may be further forged into other shapes applicable to how, when and what sort of pattern will be applied. This chapter will deal mainly with the reduction of the billet to a patternable sheet of metal. Other patterning techniques are dealt with in more detail in Chapter 11.

Forging and rolling hot metals can be dangerous, particularly when using powered hammers and rollers, which are especially dangerous pieces of machinery. Those who are inexperienced in their use will require tutelage, and all users must be aware of safety procedures. When forging, always wear protective, non-flammable clothing covering arms, legs and feet – a leather apron is good. Always wear ear protection, gloves and if so desired, a face visor. When power rolling, never feed the metal into the mill by hand; always use a wooden push rod – do not use metal tongs or pliers. Do not take hold of the metal as it comes out of the mill: a billet can suddenly curl and trap your hand. Keep hair away from rotating machinery.

Of all the procedures in the manufacture of mokumé, the deformation of the billet remains the area most subject to practical experience; this is demonstrated by the wide variety of methods used by different practitioners for preparing and forging the billet[1]. The control

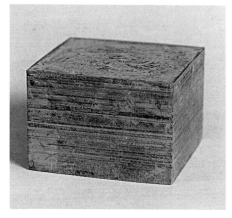

Bonded billet.

1 These procedures are described in more detail in Steve Midgett's book.

and measurement of applied forces during deformation can only be estimated and is completely subjective, whether using a machine or a hand hammer. In forging a mokumé billet, only one constant is agreed upon by all makers; although the billet may look perfectly bonded as in photo on page 69, it still tends to behave like a lot of 'sheets of metal stuck together'. It is not until a certain stage is passed during the forging process (and anyone who has forged out a mokumé billet will have observed it), that the 'sheets stuck together' suddenly become an integral sheet or block of metal.

Depending on the hardness or size of the billet, it will be necessary to decide whether to forge by hand or mechanically. I have found that the precision and evenness of power hammering gives the best results and I use that procedure for all large billets – experimental or precious metal billets are simply too small to put under a power hammer. Usually forging is carried out hot as the metals are softer, although for some metals and combinations the forging temperature can be critical. Refer to Chapters 7 and 13 for data on specific metals and combinations.

Delamination problems generally occur in the early stages of forging, before the transition phase to one sheet of metal. Delamination is generally attributable to three causes:

(a) The billet wasn't properly bonded in the first place; this usually leads to massive, multiple delamination and usually means starting again. Incomplete bonding can easily be spotted – the billet will either fall apart completely or large splits will occur suddenly, exposing oxidised metal.

(b) Incomplete bonding at the edges; a result of either oxidation creep where there has been insufficient protection from contaminating atmospheres, or 'roll-over', where the edges of the sheets are rounded by guillotining, so they do not meet. This can be limited by careful preparation of the exposed edges in the bonded billet as described later.

(c) The billet wasn't forged properly; too much force in one area can cause excess stress in another part of the billet, causing it to partially delaminate. A successful forging procedure is described later.

Delaminating billet.

Assuming that cause (a) is not a factor (the billet has been well bonded), then most problems are going to be **caused** by (b) and (c). The **reason** for these problems is a phenomenon called 'unrestricted compression stress.' Unrestricted compression stress occurs when the billet is deformed. As the hammer strikes the metal, friction tends to bind the metal in contact with hammer and anvil surfaces, restricting the flow. The metal has to go somewhere, so it bulges out at the edges, from under the hammer face. This creates shear and tension stresses in the bulging metal as shown below. The tension around the edges will exacerbate cause (b) and any incipient splits at the interfaces will open. If forged incorrectly, cause (c), this peripheral tension can actually pull apart perfectly bonded layers and cause enough delamination to render the billet useless – see photo opposite.

Billet preparation

All billets, regardless of manufacturing procedure, must have their edges prepared to minimise early delamination problems.

In the past, exponents of the traditional manufacturing technique have generally advocated trimming all the edges back to clean bonded metal, usually 3-6mm ($^1/_8$-$^1/_4$in.); this is certainly advisable when the billet has been bonded in a forge, where the atmosphere will be far from perfect. Other recommendations have included rounding off all the edges, applying solder to all the layered faces, etc. These procedures all have their merit and can be investigated by the individual craftsperson. My own personal experience has shown that splitting is minimised by making the layered faces and corners of the billet *concave*, as shown overleaf, top.

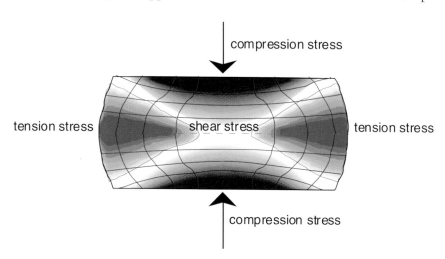

compression stress

tension stress   shear stress   tension stress

compression stress

Unrestricted compression stress.

Bonded billet prepared for forging.

This can be done by filing, or on a linisher or rotating sanding belt. The concavity need not be more than 1-2mm deep in the face of a billet 25mm thick. This causes less wastage and immediately exposes any imperfectly bonded edges, which should be further ground back as necessary. This has the effect when forging of keeping the layered faces inwards or more vertical for a time and limiting the bulging effect of unrestricted compression stress, so there is less tension pulling the layers apart.

Hand hammering

Hand forging is the traditional method of forging out a mokumé billet and the control of hammering is limited to visual and practical experience. Most copper/brass/ bronze metals can be forged red hot, but if the billet contains silver, particularly in alloy form (sterling, *shibuishi*), the billet must not be forged above black/very dark red heat. Except where used in small billets (no more than 25mm (1in.) square), I do not recommend hand forging metals such as titanium, Monel metal and stainless steel.

Heat the billet evenly with a large gas torch or in the blacksmiths forge. Use a 750 – 1000g (1½ – 2lb) hammer with a 35 – 50 mm (1½ – 2in.) very slightly crowned face, with rounded

Hand forging of billet.

edges to prevent folding of the surface. Holding the billet with a pair of tongs, place on a flat anvil and forge around the edges, working inwards to the centre (see above). Hammer gently initially. Reheat, turn over and repeat. When the billet is down to about ½-⅔ its original thickness, the forging can be directional using a curved face hammer or a large cross-peen. Patterning can commence at any stage (refer Chapter 11). The billet can be forged down to any thickness; see below for rolling procedures.

Power hammering

Like hand forging, the control of power hammering is subject to

Forging using power hammer.

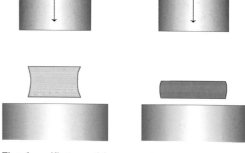

Flat face/flat anvil hammering.

visual and practical experience. The hammer can be of any reciprocating type, whether a trip, spring, or air hammer. The power of the hammer is not important, although a very powerful one will have to be used gingerly. If you are using a forge normally used for blacksmithing, clean the area. There is nothing worse than small pieces of iron scale or coke dust hammered into a mokumé surface.

Heat the billet evenly with a large gas torch or in the blacksmiths' forge, as for the hand hammering procedure. Initially the billet is flat hammered with a parallel flat hammer face on a flat anvil as shown in drawing, top right; this is to consolidate the bond between the layers. The bulging that occurs through unrestricted compression stress can be clearly seen on page 70. To minimise this stress, hammer carefully, heating and reducing in small increments, turning over frequently. It is recommended that

the billet be reduced by 25–30% of its thickness only. Any splitting that occurs in the outer edges should be ground or cut out now.

At this stage it must be decided how the billet is to be used; whether it will be twist forged, cut up and rolled into striped metal, rolled out into sheet, etc. For a sheet of metal, the billet must be thinned and stretched out to a thickness suitable for patterning. This is achieved by hammering with a cylindrically curved face hammer on a flat anvil (see page 74, bottom and this page, below); it is preferable that the curved face be attached to the striking hammer, however if this is unavailable a curved setting anvil can be used. The hammering is conducted in two steps. The first stage, below, shows the cross-hammering,

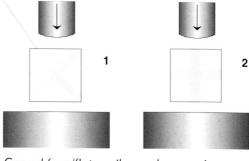

Curved face/flat anvil cross hammering.

73

which stretches the billet initially; hammer across the diagonals firstly, then parallel to the sides in the middle. Hammer gently, reheating, turning and repeating the process as many times as desired. This is necessary in order to keep the hammer blows as far from the edges as possible, minimising that old unrestricted compression stress.

By now, the billet should be thin enough to assume that if it was going to fall apart, it would have done so by now, so by parallel hammering from the edges inwards, the billet can be thinned and stretched to the required shape as shown on the right.

When forging billets containing titanium, the billet must be protected from the atmosphere. Hot titanium can absorb large amounts of oxygen, hydrogen and nitrogen, making the metal brittle and unworkable. Paint the whole billet with a thick borax paste and wrap it in a copper shim jacket, sealing all edges by folding and malleting

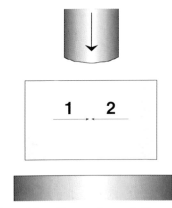

Curved face/flat anvil parallel hammering.

Billets ready for rolling and patterning.

down. When forging, the billet must not be heated above the critical annealing temperature – refer Combinations Table, Chapter 13.

Rolling

When the billet has reached the desired thickness, it can then be rolled. I recommend power rollers, particularly for large billets. The size of the rolling mill is going to limit the final size of the mokumé sheet; if you want a 300mm wide sheet of metal, then you will have to access appropriate rollers – see page 68.

Do not pickle the metal at this stage; every time you anneal and pickle the oxide is removed, allowing more exposed metal to oxidise, thinning the surface layers. Also, acid will seep into any small splits or rollovers at the edges, which will be squeezed out onto the rollers. Cleaning should be done on the last two passes through the rollers. After pickling, rinse thoroughly in boiling water with a teaspoon of sodium bicarbonate and dry with a warm flame to remove any moisture.

Always forge down the leading edge to be fed into the rollers, particularly if the billet is to be rolled fairly thick. This mitigates rolling stresses (which are similar to unrestricted compression stresses), which can cause peel-back.

The billet is passed through the rolling mills in one direction, always from the same leading edge, but turning over at each pass, until work hardening occurs. If the billet starts to curl, anneal and hammer flat. When cross rolling or changing rolling direction, always anneal and forge down the leading edge. If splitting at the leading edge starts, cut it out immediately or use a new leading edge.

Reduction between anneals should generally be no more than 20-25%. Anneal evenly with a gas/air torch, judging temperature by colour; silver alloys to dark red, copper and copper alloys to mid red, ferrous metals to very bright red, aluminium should be annealed using the burnt match method. Some annealing temperatures are critical – refer to Chapters 7 and 13 for data on specific metals and combinations.

Hot Rolling Some combinations using harder metals cannot be cold rolled, particularly while the billet is still comparatively thick and especially if they are combined with softer material. If they are rolled cold, the harder metals tend to work harden and fracture rapidly, causing failure of the sheet. Even when hot rolled, there is a tendency for them to break up – this effect can be seen in the deformed Silver-Monel metal system, page 94. This includes all combinations with iron, steel, stainless, Monel metal and titanium. Mills that are suitable for hot rolling are few and difficult to access. However an old rolling mill will suffice, provided the rolls will stand the forces. The mill should be powered. Heat the forged billet either in a kiln or with a gas/air torch to the maximum annealing temperature applicable. Using a pair of tongs, transfer the billet to the feed platform of the mill as quickly as possible, then push the billet in with a wooden push rod. Do not force the metal into the rollers; allow them to take the metal. Reheat after each pass. Reduction should be the maximum the rolling machinery can handle. Do not overheat the rollers. There will be considerable extrusion of the softer metals at the edges, but this is not a cause for concern.

By the time the rolling stage of billets containing titanium is reached, it is likely that the protective jacket will have disintegrated. Although the titanium will absorb gases when hot, because of rollover and the fact that the layers are thin, the gaseous absorption from the edges is minimal and the sheet can be trimmed back. In order to prevent the formation of intermetallics, the billet/sheet must not be heated above the critical annealing temperature – see Table, Chapter 13 .

Roller printed patterning of aluminium alloy mokumé gane.

CHAPTER 11

Patterning

Although there is no limit to the number of layers in a mokumé gane billet, experience has shown that between 8 and 40 layers is the optimum range for patterning: below 8 it is difficult to establish a pattern, and above 40 the pattern becomes too fine to see comfortably with the naked eye. The patterning techniques described here are generally applicable to rolled billets and sheet[1], and are those familiar to the author. Also described is twist patterning, which is applicable to smaller items or as applied decoration. They are by no means the sum total of possible techniques; procedures such as CAD-CAM milling and engine turning[2] are not included here. There remains only the inventiveness and creativity of the individual to expand upon existing techniques and develop new ones.

Patterning can be the most time consuming part of the process in making mokumé. It is however, also the best part. It is said that the patterning of a mokumé is a random event that cannot be controlled or repeated; this is only partly true. The overall effect and appearance of a pattern can be controlled, but the precise location of a line or layer cannot. An extra pass with the file or sanding stick and the pattern shifts; minimally, but it shifts. This is when the magic and fascination appears.

Please note: all references to combination samples refer to samples on pages 109 onwards, and references to plates refer to illustrations in the Gallery (page 114 onwards).

---

1 Some patterning techniques are only applicable in certain circumstances and are described in detail in other publications. For example, the massive twist forging of billets described by Ruth Taubmann (Metalsmith, Vol. 3, Spring 1983, p. 39) can only be applied to billets containing metals of very similar mechanical properties, such as silver/copper or copper/gilding metal.

2 These are variations of the controlled milling technique described further on; CAD-CAM is in its pioneering stage and is discussed in some detail in Steve Midgett's book, p. 98. Engine turning was used some years ago by Alistair McCallum; he obtained very precise fine patterns, which he distorted by spinning. Nowadays, CAD-CAM could be used as a substitute for engine turning.

Equipment

Perhaps the most important item in patterning is a rolling mill. Otherwise, patterning can be achieved with the minimum of equipment. For hand tools, hammers, a variety of repouseé and doming punches, carving chisels, files, etc. are all that is necessary. A flat/slightly curved steel stake and a pitch bowl to support the work. Some patterns can be applied using machinery such as a flexi-drive jeweller's drill, a milling machine or an angle grinder. A linisher is a great labour saving device as a substitute for files, but should be used with caution.

Detailed descriptions on how to use the equipment mentioned above are not included. As with all metalworking techniques, certain safety rules have to be observed. Most of the techniques detailed below involve hand tools and general studio safety practices should be followed. Some techniques involve the use of machinery; keep hair tied back and always wear safety goggles/visor, earmuffs if necessary, and wear gloves when using a grinder or linisher.

When using a powered rolling mill, push the metal into the rolls with a wooden push stick.

Patterning principles

The following essentials and rules form the basis for patterning a sheet of mokumé.

1. Applying a pattern to mokumé necessitates the removal of metal; this is generally between 15% and 33% of the metal in a billet.
2. Patterning is done basically in two ways. One way is to **emboss** the metal and then file the surface off smooth, exposing the layers. The other is to **carve** through the layers, then roll or hammer it flat to bring the exposed layers to the surface.
3. The complexity of the pattern is determined by a number of variables: the number of different metals in the billet, the number of layers in the billet, the number of layers exposed when the pattern is applied, the thickness of the

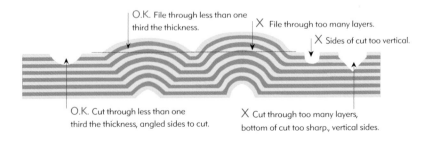

O.K. File through less than one third the thickness.

X File through too many layers.

X Sides of cut too vertical.

O.K. Cut through less than one third the thickness, angled sides to cut.

X Cut through too many layers, bottom of cut too sharp., vertical sides.

material when the pattern is applied, the number of times the pattern is applied.

4. Thinning the metal by rolling or forging will enlarge the pattern. This enlargement can be calculated and controlled proportionally.

5. Cuts or indentations into the metal should not be deeper than a third the thickness of the billet or sheet. Any deeper and there is a risk of tearing a hole, as the metal is pulled too thin when rolled or forged to an even thickness.

6. Cuts and indentations should not have sharp corners or valleys. These can cause fractures or holes in the sheet with further deformation.

7. Cuts and indentations should not have vertical sides. These can roll over during rolling or forging, which can develop into cracks and splits.

8. The pattern does not go right **through** the metal; one side can remain blank. However, once applied the pattern is **inherent** in the metal; excessive removal of material simply coarsens and reduces the pattern.

9. Patterns can be applied to both sides of the sheet, and they can be different.

Mathematics of patterning

There is a certain amount of arithmetic involved in the patterning process. If a billet has 8 layers, then the maximum depth of cut for patterning is 0.33 x 8 = 2-and-a-bit layers – not a very complex pattern. Whereas for 40 layers, 0.33 x 40 = 13; a very fine pattern. If the requirement is to only expose a certain number of layers – the depth of the cut can be calculated. For example, it may be required to expose five layers in a billet that has 25 layers. If the billet is to be patterned at 3.0mm ($\frac{1}{8}$in.) thick, then 3.0 ÷ 25 = 0.12 mm ($\frac{5}{1000}$in.) thickness for each layer: 0.12 x 5 = 0.6mm ($\frac{25}{1000}$in.), the required cutting depth. This can also be used to calculate the maximum depth of cut for a carved pattern; 3 x 0.33 = 1.0mm ($\frac{40}{1000}$in.), or 25 x 0.33 = 7 – 8 the maximum number of layers to be filed through in an embossed pattern.

It may sometimes be necessary to know beforehand the potential size of a finished sheet of metal. First calculate the volume of the billet; for example a bonded billet 50 x 50 x 30mm (2 x 2 x 1.2in.) thick has a volume of 75000mm³(4.8ins³), which can be transformed into a 3.0mm ($\frac{1}{8}$in.) thick sheet 100 x 250mm (4 x 10in.), or a 1.0mm ($\frac{40}{1000}$in.) thick sheet 300 x 250mm (12 x 10in.), or permutations thereof. However, as noted in (1.) metal has to be removed to create the pattern and it is difficult to measure that amount of metal. So it is necessary to weigh the billet before and after applying the pattern. Say for example, the before-mentioned billet weighed 1044g (36oz) before and 783g (27oz) after patterning. Therefore the volume of the billet has been reduced to 75% of the original; 0.75 x 75000 = 56250mm^3 (3.6in.^{3}), which can be rolled to a 1.0mm ($^{40}/_{1000}$in.) thick sheet 56250mm^2 – 225 x 250mm (9 x 10in.), or permutations thereof. This can also be expressed as the thickness being reduced by 75%, for example if a 3.0mm ($^1/_8$in.) thick sheet 100 x 250mm (4 x 10in.) is patterned, the nominal thickness is now 3.0 x 0.75 = 2.25mm ($^{90}/_{1000}$in.). These calculations can also be used to determine and control pattern distortion as noted in (4.). If the sheet is then reduced to 1.0mm ($^{40}/_{1000}$in.), then it will have 2.25 times the area. If the sheet is rolled in one direction only, then the pattern will enlarge 2.25 times in that direction, i.e. the sheet will be either 100 x 562mm (4 x 22.5in.), or 225 x 250mm (9 x 10in.). It may be required to keep the pattern in proportion, as in square grid or circle patterns, for example. Then the finished sheet will have to be kept to the ratio of the patterned billet. Using the same billet, the volume of the patterned billet is 56250mm^3 (3.6in^3), which can be rolled to a 1.0mm ($^{40}/_{1000}$ in.) thick sheet 56250mm^2 (90 in.^{2}) in area. The ratio of the 100 x 250 billet = 1:2.5. This forms the equation:

$$1x \times 2.5x = 56250 : 2.5 \times 2 = 56250 :$$
$$x^2 = 22500 : x = 150mm \text{ (6in.)}.$$

Therefore 2.5x = 375mm (15in.). If the billet is rolled and cross-rolled at right angles to 375 x 150 (15 x 6in.), it will maintain the proportions of the pattern.

The above calculations for pattern control are applicable to one patterning of the billet only. Because the surface layers are already disturbed, any further pattern overlay introduces complete randomness, and proportions cannot be controlled. Of course, the calculations for the finished size of the sheet can still be made; simply weigh the billet and re-calculate between pattern overlays.

Embossed patterning

Assorted patterning punches.

(a) **Bumping up**. Usually used where it is required that the metal be rolled flat after patterning. Fix the metal face down in a pitch bowl or secure to a block of soft wood. Use punches to dent the back of the metal, which will texture the face of the sheet. Because of the thickness of the metal, the raised areas on the face are ill defined and the best results are obtained using various doming punches. Cut back the raised areas on the face, taking care not to go through too many layers (page 78). Hammer or roll the sheet flat.

This pattern can be seen on pages 86 and 109.

(b) **Double bumping** up. After cutting back the face, roll the sheet flat and repeat the process. Because the sheet is thinner, the pattern will be finer and it will be completely disordered. Another way is to bump up again *between* the previous dents and cut back the face again. Care must be taken not to go through too many layers.

This pattern can be seen on the frontispiece, or plate 1, (left) or page 48.

(c) **Repousseé**. A variation on bumping up, the repousseé technique is suitable for thinner sheets of metal, 0.5-1.2mm (24 – 16gge) thick. Repousseé can be used to create patterns with an overall precision, with fine irregularity in the detail. Because the metal is already thin, further rolling may not be feasible and this process is more applicable to objects where the back is covered. Fix the metal face down into a pitch block and repousseé as desired using varied punches – a selection of punches is shown on page 76. Lines, circles, crosses, images, etc. can be produced. File off

the face of the metal, taking care not to file through too many layers; use a magnifier if necessary. Planish the face flat and add to or alter the pattern if required.

This pattern can be seen on plates 16, 18 and 21 and on page 48.

(d) **Punching**. This technique is suitable for metals from 1.2mm to 5.0mm (16 – 4gge) thick and is ideal for patterning both sides of a sheet of mokumé. If it is intended to pattern both sides of the sheet, the minimum thickness is 1.8 – 2mm (13 or 12gge). The pattern will always be a precise reflection of the punches and the way they are used, yet there is a random quality in the way the layers are exposed. The size of the punches and their shape will determine the fineness and definition of the pattern – repoussé punches are ideal. A selection of punches is shown opposite.

Punch patterning.

The flow or direction of the pattern can be controlled by

punching in lineal, radial, four square, star shaped, etc. designs. Place the metal face up on a steel stake and punch the desired pattern into the surface with selected punches, taking care not to punch too deeply. This is a time-consuming process, but the result is well worth it. Lightly dish the metal with the embossed surface on the convex side. File or grind off the surface evenly. Do not remove too much material, or the pattern will coarsen and the sheet will become too thin. Roll or hammer the sheet to remove deeper punch marks and to reduce or even out the thickness.

This pattern can be seen on plates 1, (right), 2 (left), 4, 6, 12 (outside) and on page 48.

(e) **Roller printing**. This technique permits very precise pattern control, and is ideal for putting imagery and graphics into mokumé. The metal should be 0.5 – 1.5mm (24 – 14gge) thick. Etch the required pattern in **reverse** into a sheet of metal that is harder than the mokumé. Pass both sheets through the rollers, embossing the pattern into the sheet of mokumé – see page 76. Power rollers are very useful here. Grind or file off the raised surface of the embossed metal, exposing the layers. Randomness can be introduced by removing material unevenly, or repeating the process.

This pattern can be seen on page 76, and on plate 20 and on page 48.

Carved patterning

Carved patterning basically involves cutting into the surface through the layers and then rolling or hammering the metal flat to bring the exposed layers to the surface.

(f) **Chiselling**. This is the traditional Japanese way of applying a pattern to mokumé. The metal is carved, forged flat and carved again, as many times as necessary. The billet can be carved at any stage, but if it is thicker, the cuts will have to be deeper to cut through the layers. The chisel should be what is called a bull-nose, which has a rounded, curved bottom; this cuts a U-shaped groove in the metal (see page 78). The chisel can be made out of 6mm ($\frac{1}{4}$in.) square or round tool steel, and tempered and sharpened in the same way as an engraver. Secure the billet, either in a vice or to a piece of hardwood and mount that in the vice. Always chisel towards yourself; it is easier to control the chisel that way. Roll or hammer the metal flat, bringing the exposed layers to the surface. Repeat as required.

This pattern can be seen on plate 5.

(g) **Burring**. Suitable for metal 1.5 – 5.0mm (14 – 4gge) thick. A variation on chiselling, but using a round cutting burr in a flexi-drive jeweller's drill. The size of the burr will determine the fineness and depth of the cut; 5 – 10mm ($\frac{3}{16}$–$\frac{3}{8}$in.) are recommended. Wear earmuffs and a visor (the noise is horrendous and metal flies in all directions). Keep a good grip on the handpiece; the burr tends to dig in and that can cut through too many layers. Because of this, although the overall pattern design can be controlled, the manual control of the hand piece results in variegations. The depth of the cut should not be more than half the diameter of the burr; otherwise the edges of the cut can become vertical (see page 78). Roll or hammer the metal flat, bringing the exposed layers to the surface.

This pattern can be seen on plates 2 (right), 7, 23, 24, 25, and on page 48.

(h) **Controlled milling.** Suitable for thicknesses down to 3mm (8gge), this technique is ideal for producing precise geometric patterns. These patterns can distort in a fascinating manner when a flat sheet is raised or spun. There are two types of milling machines, the horizontal (with a

Controlled milled copper/gilding metal sheet.

horizontal spindle) and the turret (with a vertical spindle); which is more versatile. The cutter used must be of the bull-nose type to cut U-shaped recesses, which must be no deeper than one third the thickness of the billet; and the cutter diameter must be more than twice the proposed depth of the cut, otherwise the edges can become vertical (see page 78). Secure the billet in the milling machine. Increments between cuts (in either direction) must be exactly the same; of course randomness can be introduced deliberately. It is better to make the full depth of the cut in one pass, moving the table slowly. Keep the work as clear of swarf as possible as this can be smeared back into the cut, only to reappear and flake off during rolling. A finished sheet can be seen below left and plate 8 shows the same sheet formed into a bowl.

The same techniques can be seen on plates 10, 11, 12 (inside), 26, and on page 48.

(i) **Random milling.** A variation on the above, this technique can only be done using a turret mill. Although it may appear dangerous, it is not if the steps are followed. Screw or nail the billet to a large piece of hardwood; it must be long enough to be gripped securely with both hands to provide leverage and keep hands well clear of the cutter. Wear gloves. Place the block of wood on the milling table and adjust the cutter to machine to the required depth; lock the cutter in this position. Start the mill and holding the wood, securely guide the

Random milling.

billet into the cutter. The cutter will tend to veer off in any direction it chooses, and it will move randomly. It requires some strength to hold onto, but with a good grip on the wooden block the cutting head can generally be steered in the desired direction. Because the cutter is always biting into the metal, it is impossible to steer smoothly; and this adds randomness to the pattern. Also, because the cutter is locked into position, it is impossible for it to seize into the billet or go all the way through it.

This pattern can be seen on the front cover, and also on plates 15, 17, and page 48.

(j) **Angle grinding**. Suitable for billets that are thicker than 5mm ($^3/_{16}$in.). This technique when applied to a thick billet will create a large pattern with a painterly quality to it. Screw or nail the billet to a block of wood and mount in a vice.

Attack the billet with an angle grinder! Use good quality discs to minimise grinding abrasive into the metal. Hammer or roll flat and repeat if required. Ground in abrasive particles may have to be removed by filing.

This pattern can be seen on plates 3, 22 and 27.

Variations

There are endless variations where one type of patterning can be used to overlay another, as in the fine silver/copper on page 48, where a bumped up pattern has been overlayed by a punched flower pattern. Similarly, by varying the thickness of the layers a different effect can be achieved, for example plate 29 on page 123 has the same punched pattern on both sides, but the colour accent is changed by altering the relative thickness of the layers; the gilding metal layers are twice as thick as the fine silver on the outside, and half as thick on the inside, i.e. their relative thicknesses are reversed.

Twist forging

Patterning by twist forging is a quite different approach to the techniques mentioned above in that all the layers, i.e. the whole piece of metal is used to create a pattern, which can look like a twisted rope, or a star

Twist forging.

twist can be put into the bar. Solder, file or grind out any splits or folds that may appear. Random filing into the bar will introduce variegations into the pattern. When finished twisting, the bar may be rolled or forged back into a square bar, exposing the rope pattern. It can be drawn through a drawplate into a ring profile, etc. The photo below shows the forged bar rolled square,

pattern. Because of the procedure, this process is generally limited to use in fairly small items, usually jewellery or as applied decoration[3]. Because of the massive stresses applied during this process, the metals in the combination should have similar mechanical properties.

After the billet has been forged down, pass it through the rollers to flatten the surface. The final thickness of the billet will determine the size of the patterned metal, but in any case, should not be less than 6mm. Using a hacksaw or (preferably) a bandsaw, cut a strip from the billet that is as wide as the billet is thick, i.e. a square bar. Forge down the ends and taper to prevent splitting and roll the bar to make even and smooth. Bevel the edges. Fix one end into a vice and hold the other with a pair of tongs or multi-grips. Heat the bar with a torch to annealing temperature and slowly twist as shown above. The positioning of the flame will determine how much

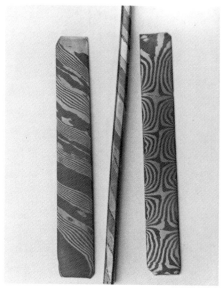

Twist forged patterns in brass/gilding metal.

and how, when the bar is then cut in half lengthwise, a swirling star pattern from the inside is exposed – obviously on one side only.

3 Steve Midgett describes in detail the making of a twist-forged bracelet. There are also several images showing star and rope patterns. Several variations on a simple twist are possible, such as reverse, tapered and herringbone twisting. These methods are discussed in more detail in *Update: mokumé gane* by Eugene and Hiroko Pijanowski.

Shield Brooch, 55mm, Ø925,
silver, Monel, copper/Monel,
mokumé gane (etched).

Shield Brooch, 52mm, Ø925,
silver, Monel, copper/Monel,
mokumé gane.

Shield Brooch,
55mm, Ø925, silver,
copper/Monel, mokumé gane.

The same sheet of copper/Monel metal mokumé gane made these three brooches.

CHAPTER 12

Colouring & patination

The final stage in the making of a piece of mokumé is the finishing and (if so desired) colouring of the surface. The success of a work often hinges on getting it just right. Sometimes subtlety is more effective than contrast: practicality and maintenance versus the effect must be considered. The techniques described here are those that have been tried and tested by the author. They are by no means the sum total of possible techniques, and there is a vast wealth of information to draw on[1]. When the number of mokumé combinations is multiplied by the number of colouring techniques, it remains only for the individual to explore the myriad of possibilities.

Safety regulations should be followed for the storage and safe, environmentally appropriate disposal of all chemicals described in this chapter. The chemicals used for etching metals are for the most part either toxic or dangerous: particular care must be paid to the safe mixing, handling and use of these acids. The chemicals used for colouring metals are generally safer, although some are hazardous and must be handled with care. Wear protective aprons, gloves, visors, etc. as necessary; ensure adequate ventilation and protection from fumes.

Finishing

Mokumé layers are often of different hardnesses and the softer material tends to wear away more during finishing. This alters the pattern balance and creates an eroded and uneven appearance to the surface. A flat surface can be maintained by sanding the filed metal with various grades (240 down to 600–1200) of wet and dry paper fixed to emery sticks. Where the relative hardnesses of the layers are very disparate, a really flat surface can be achieved with Water of Ayre stone; this is very labour

---

1 For example, Richard Hughes and Michael Rowe's book includes some 220 recipes for the patination of non-ferrous metals.

intensive, but worth the effort.

There are basically two surface finishes applicable to mokumé:

Smooth. As a rule, a high polish finish is not generally recommended because the reflective surface tends to confuse the eye and detract from the main attribute of mokumé, namely its pattern. A matt or soft semi-matt surface is the best finish for mokumé. This brings out the pattern and the true colours of the metal to their advantage. Also when the metal has to be further coloured, it provides an excellent key for the patina. A fine matt surface can be achieved by finishing with pumice and a wet cloth. There are various grades of synthetic scouring pads such as Scotchbrite, which produce a range of matt finishes; these can be used with or without pumice. Other techniques include glass brushing and bead or sand blasting (which is very matt). If a more satin or semi-matt surface is required, use a soft brass brush with soap and water.

Rules are meant to be broken, and where one (hard) metal is reflective and the other (softer) is not, an interesting optical illusion can be obtained where one colour seems to float above the other reflective surface (see page 86, middle brooch). Also, to obtain the most vibrant colours in anodised aluminium mokumé, it should be polished. After using the Water of Ayre stone, polish the surface with 1200 silicon carbide

wet and dry, using it wet. Do not use pumice on aluminium, as it tends to grind into the metal.

Etched. Certain chemicals or mordants can be used to differentially etch mokumé, either to lightly texture the surface, or completely alter its appearance. The result depends on a number of variables – the mordants used, their strength, the combination of metals in the mokumé, and the length of time they are etched.

The work should be finished as described previously: most mordants will actually enlarge and emphasise imperfections such as scratches, etc. Ensure that the surface is clean. Mask all areas to remain un-etched with plastic contact film or bitumen stop-out. Support the work on a plastic frame or trivet and lower into the mordant. Agitate the bath if necessary and use a feather or soft plastic brush to clear away bubbles. Remove the work from time to time, rinse and check the surface. Repeat until desired depth or effect is reached. Do not over-etch, as the mordant can undercut layers, lifting off small pieces and creating sharp edges. After etching, rinse and neutralise the metal in a boiling solution of sodium bicarbonate. The mokumé may now be patinated as required. If a satin sheen is required, brush with a soft brass brush and soap and water.

The mordants listed below give an introduction to the various reactions and effects that can be achieved.

Aqua Regia. This acid is the only etchant for gold; it will differentially attack various alloys, particularly of different karat. It severely attacks all other metals apart from platinum, palladium, titanium and niobium and its use is limited. A mixture of 75% full strength hydrochloric and 25% full strength nitric, this is a fuming acid and is very dangerous. Aqua regia must be mixed at least 24 hours before use.

Nitric Acid (HNO_3). Use at 30-50% maximum strength; if the reaction is too vigorous it will give off nitrous oxide fumes, which are poisonous. This acid will etch non-ferrous metals, and in order of increasing severity, Monel metal, silver, copper, gilding metal, brass. Page 86 shows a copper/Monel metal mokumé where the copper is completely etched away and the Monel is only slightly etched. Page 48 shows a copper/titanium mokumé where the copper is completely etched away and the titanium is untouched.

Hydrochloric Acid (HCl). Use at 30-50% strength; this acid will etch ferrous metals, and in order of increasing severity, nickel, Monel metal, stainless steel, iron. It will also etch silver and copper very slowly, but it will attack the zinc content of brass vigorously.

Ferric Chloride ($FeCl_3$). The safest of the mordants, it has much the same effect on non-ferrous metals and alloys as nitric acid, but etches more slowly. Ferric Chloride also etches aluminium, stainless steel and iron.

Hydrofluoric Acid (HFl). The only mordant that will etch titanium and niobium, this acid is particularly dangerous. To brighten the surface it is usually used as a mix; one part full strength hydrofluoric, one part full strength nitric and 1-2 parts water. Hydrofluoric (by itself) does not attack silver, copper or ferrous metals.

Sodium Hydroxide (NaOH). Used as a solution of 150 g/l (24 oz/gal.) in water, this mordant will differentially etch aluminium alloys. The reaction gives off hydrogen gas, which is flammable.

Colouring

When mokumé was invented 300 years ago, the Japanese had already developed sophisticated techniques for the patination of metals, particularly the extensive range of non-ferrous alloys used in decorative metalwork. The earliest mokumé examples are of copper and shakudo, which in their natural state are almost the same colour, so without patination the pattern would be meaningless. Since then, all mokumé in Japan has generally been patinated with Rokusho.

With all combinations it is firstly a necessary decision as to whether the metal should be further coloured or not. Some metals are unstable in air and can either erode or develop erratic and undesirable colours; patination can stabilise a metal surface and control the colour. On the other hand patination may be undesirable where there is the risk of damage to the surface coating, as in a high use or wear situation such as utensils, rings, etc. In this case of course, the combination must be not only corrosion resistant, but present an acceptable colour contrast.

Considerations when choosing a patination procedure for a mokumé combination are:

What affect the patina has on all the metals in the combination, i.e. their stability and colour (aesthetically and compatibly).

If multiple patinas are used, the sequence of subsequent applications and what effect they will have on preceding patinas.

The surface finish influences the effect of a patina. Patinas generally do not take well to highly polished surfaces and any variation in the texture can alter the effect. The surface of the work should be finished as desired, whether smooth or etched. The surface to be patinated must be perfectly clean and dry; any contaminants will affect the result. Patination procedures are generally critical in their composition and application; some recipes can be very erratic in their performance and it may require several attempts to attain the desired result. If the procedure does not work, clean back to the metal and re-finish again. The following recipes/procedures are guidelines only. Important safety issues are noted. The prefix letter is cross referenced in the second bracket to the images captions.

a) **Natural finish.** Generally the work is sanded with 600 grit silicon carbide wet & dry and cleaned with pumice and a soft brush.

This patination can be seen in combination samples 1–28(a), pages 109–113, plates 1, 2 (left), 6 (outside), 25 and also on page 48.

b) **Vapour.** The work is suspended/supported in a sealed container containing ammonia. Concentrated ammonia is a severe irritant to the mucous membranes, lungs and eyes; avoid contact with the vapour. To dispose of, rinse away with copious amounts of water. Household ammonia (6%) may be substituted, but it is slower acting and of less reliable performance.

This patination can be seen in combination samples 2–4 (c), 10(b)–13 (c), 15 (b), 20–22 (c), 26 (b), 31 and on plates 3, 5, 8, 9, 13, 17, 18,21, 22 and on page 48.

c) **Vapour.** Saturate a concentrated ammonia solution with salt. Treat work as above (b).

This patination can be seen on combination samples 18(c) and 23(c).

d) **Solution**. Rokusho is the traditional Japanese patination for mokumé. Obtainable only in Japan, its exact composition is unknown. Use either a copper or ovenproof glass container; if using a glass one, a copper rod must also be suspended in the solution. Bring to a rolling boil a solution of:

4 gm *Rokusho*
4 gm Copper Sulphate
1 litre of water
1 *Umeboshi* (pickled) plum

After cleaning, the work is covered with grated *daikon* (also called mooli or white Chinese radish) for several minutes. Clear away the *daikon* (do not rinse) and suspend the work in the simmering solution for 30-60 minutes.
This patination can be seen on page 86 (centre) and plates 4, 14 and on page 48.

e) **Solution**. Heat to 80°C (175°F) a solution of:
125g copper nitrate
72.5g copper sulphate
72.5g salt
litre of water
Suspend the work in the hot solution for 15-20 minutes.
This patination can be seen on combination samples 5(b), 8(c), 16 (b) .

f) **Solution.** Bring to a rolling boil a solution of:
125g copper sulphate
50g sodium chlorate
1 litre of water

Suspend the work in the simmering solution for 15 – 20 minutes.
This patination can be seen on samples 1(c), 4(b), 5(c), 15(c).

g) **Solution.** Heat to 80°C (175°F) a solution of:

125g copper carbonate.
50ml ammonia
1 litre of water

Suspend the work in the hot solution for 15 – 20 minutes.
This patination can be seen on samples 6(c), 8(b), 14(c), 16(c), 19(c), 21(b), 22(b), 24(b), 25(c).

h) **Solution.** Heat to 80°C (175°F) a solution of:

5g potassium polysulphide (liver of sulphur)
1 litre of water

Suspend the work in the hot solution for 1 – 5 minutes. The solution gives off Hydrogen Sulphide gas which, in high concentration, is poisonous.
This patination can be seen on combination samples 7(b), 8(c), plates 6 (inside), 12, 19.

i) **Solution.** Put potassium nitrate in a stainless steel container and heat over a gas ring until the powder melts. This solution is molten at 380°C (710°F) and is dangerous if not handled carefully. Do not get any inflammable substances (such as oil) in it, as it will catch fire. Do not get any water in it, as this turns instantly to steam and blows the molten solution in all directions. Do not immerse closed hollow objects. The solution will appear cloudy at first; when this clears it is ready. Make sure the work is completely dry. Hold the work with tweezers, or tongs, wires, etc. so marks will not show. Heat with a soft flame until an even flash of oxide colour appears over the work (this also has the advantage of ensuring that it is dry) and suspend in the solution for one to three minutes. Remove and rinse immediately under hot running water. When finished, allow the solution to cool; it will solidify, but it can be re-heated and re-used indefinitely.

This patination can be seen on combination samples 1–3(b), 7(c), 10–14(b), 17(b), 20(b), 24(c), 26(c), 27(b), 28(c) and plates 7, 10, 15, 28 and on page 48.

j) **Solution.** Heat the work to red/orange temperature and immerse immediately in machine oil, moving it about. Remove and wash off oil with turpentine then detergent and water.

This patination can be seen on combination samples 28(b) and plate 16.

k) **Heat**. Heat the work to red/orange temperature and plunge into hot water. Repeat twice. This is good for colouring Monel metal, as it can then be pickled without removing the black patina, allowing use of another patina on the other metals in the combination.

This patination can be seen on page 86 (bottom), and combination samples 6(b), 17(c).

l) **Heat.** Heat the work to the desired temperature to induce interference oxidation colouring in a kiln or with a soft gas flame.

This patination can be seen on combination samples 8, 9(b), 20(b), 25(b), 27(c), 28(c) and on plates 11, 19 and on page 48.

m) **Anodising**. Aluminium alloys are anodised using the following procedure: The work is polished and stripped in a Sodium Hydroxide solution, then de-smutted in a 20% Nitric Acid bath. It is then rinsed and anodised in a 20% Sulphuric Acid bath, using a direct current of approximately 12 V and 2-3 amps/100 cm2 (4 sq in.). Finally it is rinsed and dyed using proprietary dyes and sealed in a steam vapour cabinet.

This patination can be seen on the front cover, page 76, combination samples 29 and 30 and on plates 2 (right), 20, 23, 26 and page 48.

And finally...

Although patinas stabilise and colour a metal surface, they are sometimes susceptible to further atmospheric degradation.

When the piece of work is finally finished, it is advisable to protect patinated surfaces with a wax coating. Silicon wax, a carnauba style hard setting furniture wax or beeswax is suitable. Apply the wax and buff off with a soft cloth. This procedure should be repeated at least once a year. Excess wax can be removed with white spirit or turpentine.

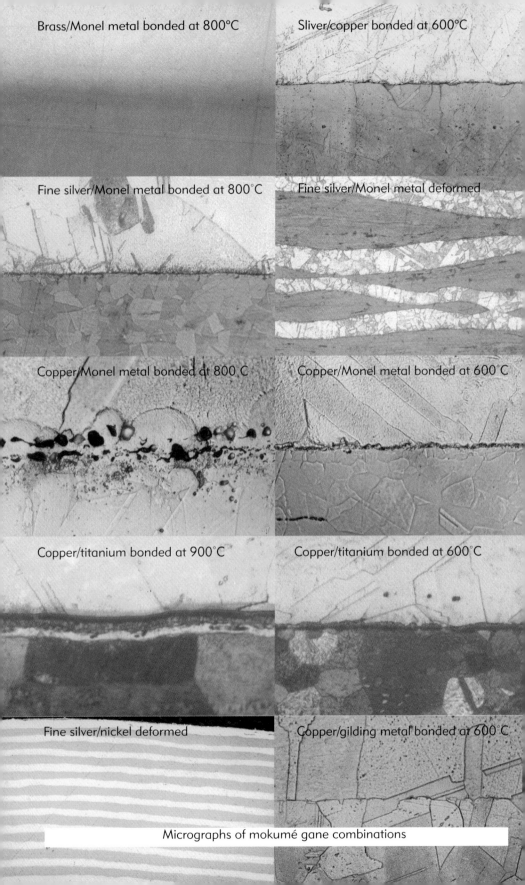

Brass/Monel metal bonded at 800°C

Sliver/copper bonded at 600°C

Fine silver/Monel metal bonded at 800°C

Fine silver/Monel metal deformed

Copper/Monel metal bonded at 800°C

Copper/Monel metal bonded at 600°C

Copper/titanium bonded at 900°C

Copper/titanium bonded at 600°C

Fine silver/nickel deformed

Copper/gilding metal bonded at 600°C

Micrographs of mokumé gane combinations

CHAPTER 13

Combinations

The diffusion bonding of dissimilar metals is a complex subject – there are approximately 67 pure metals which could be solid state diffusion bonded together. A large number of these metals are either prohibitively expensive, rare, are too similar, or require such sophisticated treatment as to render them useless or pointless to the average metalsmith. An examination of the periodic tables show that, excluding toxic, noxious, radioactive, highly flammable and highly crystalline substances, there are 21 pure metals which would satisfy the major criterion of mokumé gane; namely malleability. A simple binary combination of all these metals would theoretically give 231 possible variations. Add to this all the permutations possible using alloys and combinations of alloys, then the range of mokumé gane combinations becomes legion, and in a large number of cases, rather esoteric.

The bonding of metals is not dependent on their mutual diffusion, as those with very low mutual solubility can be joined. There are several phenomena to be considered when bonding dissimilar metals:[1]

(a) High mutual solubility favours the dispersal of oxide films after initial breakdown – see the brass/Monel metal system opposite.

(b) Solubility and diffusivity can be influential in the formation of intermetallic phases. Intermetallics are usually brittle, crystalline substances, which can cause delamination. The copper/titanium system opposite clearly shows intermetallics and the influence of temperature on their formation.

(c) Solubility and diffusivity can be influential in the formation of eutectic melts and low temperature phases, which can affect the thermal performance of a bonded system – see page 36.

(d) The disparate diffusion rate of one metal in another at a diffusion couple can cause

---

1 *AWS Welding Handbook,* 7th ed., p. 33..

porosity at the joint interface through the Kirkendall effect, as shown in the copper/Monel metal system page 94.

Not only are diffusion characteristics important, it is important that the craftsperson who intends to bond a combination of metals has a full understanding of what they will do at temperature and after they are bonded. This basically means that he or she should be able to interpret the phase diagrams of the metals involved and the significance of full understanding of diffusion parameters cannot be underestimated[2]. This can get complicated if there are a lot of metals present in the alloys, and the control of temperature requires the consideration of several thermodynamic characteristics of the metals to be joined. These include:

(e) The solidus and liquidus temperatures of all the metals and alloys involved.
(f) The solidus, liquidus and eutectic points of alloys that may be formed at the interface.
(g) The phase transformations that may occur in an alloy as temperature changes.
(h) The yield strength of the metals at temperature.

A simple example of this is shown in the silver/copper phase diagram – opposite. It can be seen that at room temperature, an alloy of silver and copper is composed of two phases, alpha which is silver with a tiny amount of copper dissolved in it, and beta which is copper with a tiny amount of silver dissolved in it. When they solidify, these two alloys interlock in a dendritic pattern, which is why alloys such as shibuishi are so tough and work-harden so rapidly. The diagram also shows that there is a eutectic alloy formed at 28.5% Cu in Ag, which melts at 778°C. In reality, this eutectic point is also a solidus line and for any alloy containing between 8.8% and 92% Cu, there is the formation of liquid phases in the metal above 778°C[3]. That is, any alloy of silver and copper within that range becomes unstable above that temperature, and that **any** mokumé gane combination with silver and copper present in quantity should not be heated above 778°C.

Generally, the ideal temperature range for solid state diffusion bonding is 0.5 – 0.78Tm where Tm is the lower melting point, in °Kelvin[4], of the metals to be joined. For example using the phase diagram opposite, and assuming the

2 The most important phase diagram references (of several) are: Massalski, T.B. (ed.), *Binary Alloy Phase Diagrams* and Villiers P., Prince A., Okamoto H.; *Handbook of Ternary Alloy Phase Diagrams.*
3 It is no accident that Sterling Silver is only 7.5% copper - as the phase diagram shows, it has a much higher solidus point.
4 *AWS Welding Handbook*, 7th ed., p. 318.

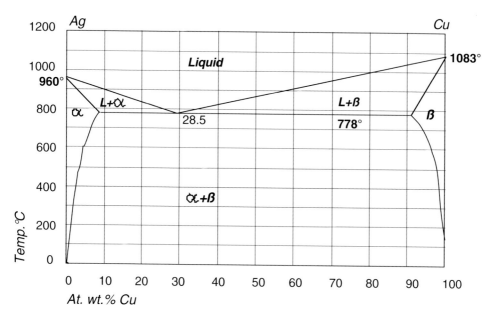

Silver/copper phase diagram.

eutectic/solidus of 778°C for copper
and silver is taken as the critical
temperature. Therefore, taken in
conjunction with the above
mentioned formula: 778°C + 273 =
1051°K x 0.5 – 0.7 = 525-735°C as the
optimum bonding range for copper
and silver. Therefore, it is feasible to
solid-state diffusion bond full-size
billets of traditional
copper/silver/gold alloys at 600°C,
well below the critical
eutectic/solidus point of 778°C.

Finally, other factors that must be
taken into account are the
mechanical and chemical
compatibilities of the metal
combination when bonded:

(i) Can it be successfully deformed
into a usable product and in what
form can it be used.

(j) Is there a significant differential
in the working properties of the
laminates – in some
circumstances, harder layers will
disintegrate and the metal will
not be a true mokumé (see the
deformed fine silver/Monel metal
system on page 94.

(k) Is the metal combination stable;
i.e. will they corrode or
disintegrate with time in a
normal environment.

(l) Is there a significant differential
in the colour combination; can
the metals be successfully
patinated to provide a
differentiation and are those
patinas stable.

An example of this can be observed
in the Compatibility Table. There are
few mentions of the metal niobium
because it requires special
conditions (preferably a vacuum) for

bonding and annealing. Although it can be coloured with heat, the best results are obtained by using an anodic electrolytic process and in all cases _except_ when combined with titanium and tantalum, the other metal in the combination will interfere with the electric field (and therefore the colouring process) and more than likely, corrode badly. This also applies when aluminium is combined with other metals – see combination samples 30 and 31.

The following information discusses the characteristics of various combinations attempted so far. The Metals Table in Chapter 8 shows the thermodynamic characteristics of the various metals used, while the Combinations Table in this chapter gives the bonding parameters of successful metal combinations, with comments on any special treatment required; also included are the bonding parameters for further untried combinations, which have been calculated from the relevant phase diagrams. This table is by no means comprehensive, and there are many other combinations that can be made. The following Compatibility Table gives a quick, overall guide to the general behaviour of various combinations.

Note: The combination samples on pages 109–113 show a comparative visual representation of 31 combinations.

However, if the correct bonding parameters cannot be determined, do not do it!

Gold/gold
Bond Temp. 700°C

Made with 920 yellow gold and 750 (18k) platinum white gold. Although easy to bond, some gold alloys have quite disparate working characteristics, so care has to be taken when deforming them. Gold mokumé alloys have been made successfully using the traditional process, and they have also been commercially produced in Japan by Mitsubishi Gold.

Gold/platinum
Bond Temp. 700°C

Made with 920 yellow gold and 950 platinum (in small quantities). Because of the disparate hardnesses, there is some extrusion of the gold at the edges. Ideal for jewellery, with a strong colour contrast.

Gold/palladium
Plate 1 and page 48. Bond Temp. 700°C

Made with 920 yellow gold and 950 palladium (in small quantities). Softer than gold/platinum, it can be readily raised, but work hardens quickly. Ideal for jewellery, with a strong colour contrast – the palladium is slightly darker than platinum.

Gold/fine silver
Plate 2. Bond Temp. 600°C

The metals in this combination when alloyed form a solid solution, they have a great affinity for one another and diffuse into one another readily. This means that over annealing and over heating can cause rapid alloying and Kirkendall porosity between the layers. The natural colour differentiation is not strong, but the silver can be blackened to give a strong contrast.

Palladium/fine silver

Plate 2. Bond Temp. 600°C

Made with 950 palladium. Ideal for jewellery, with a strong colour contrast – the metals, being inert, can be used in their natural state. Platinum/fine silver would be similar.

Fine silver/copper

Combination sample 1, plates 3, 4, 27 and page 48. Bond Temp. 650°C

This is one of the classic traditional combinations. The metal is very malleable and the silver and copper have similar mechanical properties, which allows for heavy deformation and patterning of the metal; it can easily be twist forged and rolled as striped metal. Although the silver has a limited colour range, the copper can be patinated a number of colours.

Note: In all the combinations listed above and below (excluding Monel metal, iron and stainless steel), 925 sterling silver can be substituted for fine, which will make the metal tougher and it may be more physically compatible, but it must be forged at black heat to prevent crumbling of the sterling silver, which in turn may present annealing problems. Care must be taken with the sterling silver layers as they are subject to fire-stain when annealed;

because the layers are very thin, fire-stain can go right through the layer. The new proprietary fire stain resistant 'Bright Silver'[5] has been used successfully, but it has several low temperature characteristics and care must be taken when soldering and annealing.

Fine silver/shibuishi

Combination sample 2, plates 3, 18 and page 48. Bond Temp. 650°C

Must be hammered at black heat; shibuishi is very tough and work hardens very quickly so it must be annealed frequently. Because of the disparate hardness's, there is considerable extrusion of soft silver at the edges. Dependent on grade of shibuishi, a wide range of colours can be attained.

Fine silver/shakudo

Combination sample 3. Bond Temp. 650°C

This is one of the classic traditional combinations. The metal is very malleable and the silver and shakudo have similar mechanical properties, which allows for heavy deformation and patterning of the metal; it can easily be twist forged and rolled as striped metal. Increasing the percentage of gold up to 10% can change the colour of the shakudo to purple when coloured with Rokusho; however this colour can also be obtained with ordinary shakudo by patinating it in molten potassium nitrate (see Chapter 12).

5 *This metal contains a small amount of germanium, which prevents the formation of fire stain*

Fine silver/gilding metal

Combination sample 2, plates 5, 18, 21, 24, 27 and page 48. Bond Temp. 650°C

The low zinc content of gilding metal mitigates against the formation of low temperature phases and also makes it malleable enough to behave much as silver/copper. As it can be patinated black with ammonia vapour, gilding metal can sometimes be used as a substitute for shakudo. With this combination, if it is left in the ammonia vapour long enough, the silver will patinate bright blue.

Fine silver/brass

Combination sample 4. Bond Temp. 600°C

This combination has a critical bonding and annealing temperature – any heating above 650°C is likely to cause the formation of low temperature phases, which are basically silver solder!

Fine silver/nickel

Plates 6 and 23, and page 48.
Bond Temp. 800°C

This combination is very malleable, but as the metals are insoluble within each other, over annealing can cause minor delamination of patterned layers. It is also very soft in its annealed state and should be used quite thick or in the work-hardened state. Although it is a very pleasing combination to work and has attractive natural colours, because of the known carcinogenic properties of nickel, it must be handled with care and used with discretion.

Fine silver/nickel silver

Combination sample 5. Bond Temp. 800°C

This combination works best with 18% grade nickel silver. With a similar colour to the above combination, it is considerably tougher and requires power hammering to deform it; there is considerable extrusion of silver at the edges. This combination is also successful using 925 silver.

Fine silver/Monel metal

Combination sample 6. Bond Temp. 800°C

A tough metal, it requires power hammering to deform it, and due to the disparate working properties of the two metals, there is massive extrusion of silver at the edges and some disintegration of the Monel layers. The colour contrast in the natural state is strong, and it can be patinated several ways.

Fine silver/iron

Sample 7, and plate 7. Bond Temp. 800°C

This combination is very malleable, but quite tough, much the same as copper/iron. Care must be taken in corrosive or damp environments as there is a strong electrolytic potential between the silver and the iron; it cannot be pickled to clean it. The colour contrast in the natural state is strong, but the iron must be passivated or protected to stop it rusting.

Fine silver/stainless steel

Combination sample 8. Bond Temp. 800°C

Similar to copper/stainless steel, the resultant metal is not at all malleable; microscopic examination shows massive disintegration of stainless steel layers. In this respect, it cannot be considered a true mokumé at all, as the pattern cannot be controlled. The metal is very hard; it must be deformed red hot using a power hammer and it must be hot rolled; it requires frequent annealing, there is massive extrusion of silver at the edges and often tearing through the sheet. It presents an interesting natural disintegrated pattern and can be patinated a wide range of colours. Due to forming difficulties it is recommended to use this material in the flat form.

Note: Attempts to use 925 silver with the above three combinations have not so far been successful on a large scale – the reasons for this have not been determined.

Fine silver/titanium
Combination sample 9 and page 48. Bond Temp. 600°C

Similar to Monel metal in hardness, titanium is none the less more malleable than stainless steel, however microscopic examination shows considerable disintegration of titanium layers andin this respect, it cannot be considered a true mokumé at all. Pattern control is difficult and the bonding and annealing temperatures of this combination are critical. Over-heating causes the formation of brittle intermetallics with subsequent delamination, although the metal is very hard; it must be deformed hot (not above

600°C) using a power hammer and it must be hot rolled; it requires frequent annealing and there is massive extrusion of silver at the edges. The forming of the material presents difficulties and it cannot be shaped very far. The pattern must be applied at the final stage, as any annealing of the exposed titanium layers will prevent their colouring. It presents an interesting ragged edged pattern and the titanium can be heat coloured a wide range of colours.

925 silver/titanium
Bond Temp. 600°C

This combination is similar to the above and must be treated the same. The stronger 925 silver reduces considerably the disintegration of the titanium layers. There is the concomitant problem of fire-stain.

Shibuishi/copper
Sample 10, and plate 8. Bond Temp. 650°C

A traditional combination, it is similar to fine silver/shibuishi, it must be hammered at black heat and annealed frequently. Because of the disparate hardnesses, there is considerable extrusion of copper at the edges. Dependent on grade of shibuishi, a wide range of colours can be attained.

Shibuishi/shakudo
Combination sample 11. Bond Temp. 650°C

A traditional combination, it is similar to the above but a bit tougher; it must be hammered at black heat and annealed frequently. Dependent on grade of shibuishi, a wide range of colours can be attained.

Shibuishi/bronze
Combination sample 12. Bond Temp. 600°C

This combination has a critical bonding and annealing temperature – any heating above 650°C is likely to cause the formation of low temperature silver-tin phases, which will cause delamination. The metal is very tough; it must be deformed using a power hammer and it requires frequent and careful annealing.

Copper/shakudo
Bond Temp. 600°C

The classic traditional combination, this was the first non-ferrous mokumé gane made. The metal is very malleable and the copper and shakudo have similar mechanical properties, which allows for heavy deformation and patterning of the metal; it can easily be twist forged and rolled as striped metal. Traditionally the metal was patinated red and black when coloured with Rokusho.

Copper/gilding metal
Combination sample 13, and plates 9 and 13. Bond Temp. 650°C

One of the easiest combinations to make; it is very malleable like Silver/Copper. It can be patinated to provide a strong contrast.

Copper/brass
Combination sample 14, and plates 10, 13, and page 48. Bond Temp. 700°C

An easy combination to make, it is malleable and slightly tougher than copper/gilding metal; the colour contrast is strong.

Copper/bronze
Combination sample 15. Bond Temp. 700°C

This combination has only been attempted with tin bronze and the malleability is dependent on the tin content, as are the variations in patination. The tin content will also have a bearing on whether it can be hot forged or not. There is some extrusion of the softer copper at the edges. It is generally malleable and slightly tougher than copper/ brass.

Copper/nickel
Plates 11 and 28. Bond Temp. 700°C

This combination shows a marked diffusion of nickel into copper, which can cause Kirkendall porosity if over heated (refer copper/Monel metal system, Figure 58); for this reason it is recommended that the pressure applied during the bonding process is maintained until the temperature is below 300°C. Care must be taken when annealing. The metal is very malleable and soft in its annealed state.

Copper/nickel silver
Combination sample 16 and plate 22. Bond Temp. 700°C

A much tougher metal than copper/nickel with disparate working characteristics causing extrusion of copper at the edges. Figure 102 was deliberately over diffused, to create a hybrid alloy at the interface.

Copper/Monel metal

Sample 17 and page 86. Bond Temp. 700°C

There is a marked diffusion of nickel into copper as in the above combination, which can cause Kirkendall porosity if over heated (refer Figure 58); for this reason it is recommended that the pressure applied during the bonding process is maintained until the temperature is below 300°C. Care must be taken when annealing. The metal is very malleable but tough, requiring power hammering, and the disparate working properties causes considerable extrusion of copper at the edges. This combination can be patinated a wide range of colours.

Copper/iron

Combination sample 18 and plate 12, and page 48. Bond Temp. 800°C

This combination is very malleable, but quite tough, much the same as silver/iron. Care must be taken in corrosive or damp environments, as there is a strong electrolytic potential between the copper and the iron; it cannot be pickled to clean it. Patination techniques are limited and the iron must be passivated or protected to stop it rusting.

Copper/stainless steel

Combination sample 19 and plate 14 also page 48. Bond Temp. 850°C

This combination is not very malleable, but more so than silver/stainless steel; there is similar massive disintegration of stainless steel layers. In this respect, it cannot be considered a true mokumé at all, as the pattern cannot be controlled. The metal is very hard; it must be deformed red hot using a power hammer and it must be hot rolled; it requires frequent annealing, there is massive extrusion of copper at the edges and often tearing through the sheet. It presents an interesting natural disintegrated pattern and can be patinated a wide range of colours. Forming is difficult and not for the faint-hearted.

Copper/titanium

Combination sample 20, and plates 16, 19, also page 48. Bond Temp. 600°C

This combination is similar to the silver/titanium and must be treated the same. It is slightly stronger and there is less disintegration of the titanium layers. As with all combinations using titanium, the pattern must be applied to the finished metal and it cannot be annealed after patterning.

Gilding metal/brass

Plate 13 and page 85. Bond Temp. 700°C

An easy combination to make, it is malleable and considerably tougher than copper/gilding metal; the colour contrast is strong when patinated.

Gilding metal/nickel

Plate 17. Bond Temp. 700°C

An easy combination to make, it is very malleable and slightly tougher than copper/nickel; the colour contrast is strong when patinated.

Gilding metal/nickel silver

Bond Temp. 700°C

A much tougher metal than gilding metal/nickel, it must be annealed frequently to prevent cracking.

Brass/bronze

Combination sample 21. Bond Temp. 700°C

This combination has only been attempted with tin bronze and the malleability is dependent on the tin content, as are the variations in patination. The tin content will also have a bearing on whether it can be hot forged or not. The metal is generally malleable and tough.

Brass/nickel

Bond Temp. 700°C

There is marked diffusion of nickel into the brass and the metal must not be over-heated. Similar to copper/nickel but tougher and very malleable.

Brass/nickel silver

Combination sample 22. Bond Temp. 700°C

The metal is very hard and tough; it must be deformed red-hot using a power hammer and it requires frequent annealing. It can be patinated a wide range of colours.

Brass/Monel metal

Combination sample 23. Bond Temp. 750°C

Over-heating this combination during bonding can lead to massive diffusion at the interfaces. The metal is very tough; it must be deformed using a power hammer, it requires frequent annealing and there is considerable extrusion of brass at the edges. Once in sheet form it is very strong but quite malleable – however, raising it is not for the faint-hearted.

Brass/iron

Combination sample 24. Plate 15, also page 48. Bond Temp. 800°C

This combination behaves much the same as Brass/Monel Metal, but is considerably more malleable. Care must be taken in corrosive or damp environments as there is a strong electrolytic potential between the brass and the iron; it cannot be pickled to clean it and the iron must be passivated and protected to stop it rusting.

Brass/stainless steel

Combination sample 25. Bond Temp. 800°C

Brass and stainless steel bond surprisingly well, but the resultant metal is not very malleable and microscopic examination shows some disintegration of stainless steel layers. The metal is very hard; it must be deformed red-hot using a power hammer and it must be hot rolled; it requires frequent annealing and there is massive extrusion of brass at the edges. It can however be patterned and patinated a wide range of colours. Due to forming difficulties it is recommended to use this material in the flat form.

Bronze/nickel silver

Combination sample 26. Bond Temp. 750°C

The metal is very hard and tough; it must be deformed red-hot using a power hammer and it requires frequent annealing. It can be patinated a wide range of colours.

Nickel silver/ Monel metal
Frontispiece. Bond Temp. 750°C

The metal is very hard and tough; it must be deformed red hot using a power hammer and it requires frequent annealing, however, it can be hand raised. Its natural colours are a very stable subtle grey/cream colour combination, but by heating and pickling, the Monel metal can be patinated black.

Nickel silver/iron
Combination sample 27. Bond Temp. 750°C

The metal is very hard and tough; it must be deformed red-hot using a power hammer and it requires frequent annealing. Over-annealing can cause the migration of zinc to the grain boundaries, particularly at the interfaces, weakening the metal and causing delamination. As with all iron objects, the metal must be passivated or patinated to prevent rust.

Iron/stainless steel
Combination sample 28. Bond Temp. 800°C

Iron and stainless steel form a tenacious bond, and the resultant metal is quite malleable. The metal is very hard; it must be deformed red hot using a power hammer and it must be hot rolled; forming it is difficult and not for the faint-hearted. As with all iron objects, the metal must be passivated or patinated to prevent rust. The colour

range is limited, although the stainless steel can be heat coloured a range of interference colours.

Aluminium alloys
Combination sample 29. Plates 2, 20, 23, 26 and pages 76 and 98. Bond Temp. 450°C

Different aluminium alloys can be diffusion bonded and patterned in the same way as a mokumé. Some of the alloys are tough structural metals, which make for a stronger aluminium than those normally associated with anodisable aluminium. Although in their natural state there is little differentiation, when anodised, a colour differential becomes apparent – combination samples 29(a–d) show how different combinations have different effects. The anodising film can be coloured and shaded as desired using commercial anodising dyes. Aluminium alloys are not suitable for bonding with most other metals; firstly aluminium tends to form intermetallics with most other metals and secondly, during anodising the other metal not only corrodes, but it impedes the electrical field, preventing anodising of the aluminium – see combination samples 30 and 31.

Bonding parameters for selected mokumé gane combinations

Combination	Temp. °C	Time mins.	Atmos.	Special Remarks T = tried E = extrapolated from data
Gold/Gold	500-700	60	N_2	E	18-22ct. Use higher temp. for white gold, lower for green gold.
Gold/Platinum	650-750	60	Ar	T	18-22ct.
Gold/Palladium	650-750	60	Ar	T	18-22ct. Not as tough as Gold/Platinum.
Gold/Fine Silver	550-650	60	N_2	T	Critical temp. range. Kirkendall porosity a hazard, particularly during forming and annealing.
Gold/Copper	550-650	60	N_2	E	Critical temp. range. Kirkendall porosity a hazard as above.
Gold/Shakudo	550-650	60	N_2	E	Critical temp. range. Kirkendall porosity a hazard as above.
Gold/Titanium	600-650	30-60	Ar	E	Critical temp. range. Maintain atmosphere until cool. Do not use green gold with cadmium.
Platinum/Fine Silver	650-750	60	Ar	E	
Palladium/Fine Silver	650-750	60	Ar	T	
Fine Silver/Shibuishi	600-700	60	N_2	T	Initially disparate working properties, but when thin the Shibuishi laminae are quite malleable.
Fine Silver/Copper	600-700	60	N_2	T	
Fine Silver/Shakudo	600-700	60	N_2	T	
Fine Silver/Gilding Metal	600-700	60	N_2	T	
Fine Silver/Brass	600-650	60	N_2	T	Critical temp. range. Overheating causes formation of solder!
Fine Silver/Nickel	750-800	60	Ar	T	Metals insoluble in each other. Overheating can cause delamination. Annealed metal very soft.
Fine Silver/Monel Metal	750-800	60	N_2	T	Very disparate working properties.
Fine Silver/Iron	750-800	60	Ar	T	Metals insoluble in each other. Very malleable. Strong electrolytic potential.
Fine Silver/Stainless Steel	750-800	60	Ar	T	Very disparate working properties, stainless disintegrates.
Fine Silver/Titanium	600-650	30-60	Ar	T	Critical temp. range. Maintain atmosphere until cool. Formation of intermetallics a hazard.
Sterling Silver/Nickel	750-800	60	Ar	T	Metals insoluble in each other. Tougher than Fine Silver/Nickel
Sterling Silver/Titanium	600-650	30-60	Ar	T	Critical temp. range. Maintain atmosphere until cool. Formation of intermetallics a hazard.
Shibuishi/Copper	600-700	60	N_2	T	
Shibuishi/Shakudo	600-700	60	N_2	T	
Shibuishi/Bronze	600-650	60	N_2	T	Critical temp. range. Formation of low temp. Ag-Sn phases a hazard during deformation.
Copper/Shakudo	600-700	60	N_2	T	

Combination	Temp. °C	Time mins.	Atmos.	Special Remarks T = tried E = extrapolated from data
Copper/Gilding Metal	600-700	60	N_2	T
Copper/Brass	600-700	60	N_2	T
Copper/Bronze	650-750	60	N_2	T
Copper/Nickel	600-700	60	Ar	T	Maintain pressure to 300°C to limit Kirkendall porosity. Annealed metal very soft and malleable.
Copper/Nickel Silver	600-700	60	N_2	T
Copper/Monel Metal	600-700	60	N_2	T	Maintain pressure to 300°C to limit Kirkendall porosity. Very disparate working properties.
Copper/Iron	700-800	60	Ar	T	Very malleable. Strong electrolytic potential. Do not pickle.
Copper/Stainless Steel	700-800	60	Ar	T	Very disparate working properties, stainless disintegrates.
Copper/Titanium	600-650	30-60	Ar	T	Critical temp. range. Maintain atmosphere until cool. Formation of intermetallics a hazard.
Gilding Metal/Brass	650-750	60	N_2	T
Gilding Metal/Nickel	600-700	60	Ar	T	Maintain pressure to 300°C to limit Kirkendall porosity.
Gilding Metal/Nickel Silver	650-750	60	N_2	T
Brass/Bronze	650-750	60	N_2	T
Brass/Nickel	600-700	60	Ar	T	Maintain pressure to 300°C
Brass/Nickel Silver	650-750	60	N_2	T
Brass/Monel Metal	650-750	60	N_2	T	Maintain pressure to 300°C
Brass/Iron	750-850	60	Ar	T	Very malleable. Strong electrolytic potential. Do not pickle.
Brass/Stainless Steel	750-850	60	Ar	T	Very tough metal. Stainless tends to disintegrate.
Bronze/Nickel	600-700	60	Ar	E	Maintain pressure to 300°C
Bronze/Nickel Silver	650-750	60	N_2	T
Bronze/Iron	700-800	60	Ar	E
Bronze /Stainless Steel	700-800	60	Ar	E
Nickel/Iron	800-900	60	Ar	E
Nickel Silver/Iron	700-800	60	Ar	T
Iron/Stainless Steel	800-900	60	Ar	T	Workable red hot only.
Titanium/Niobium	950-1150	60	Vacuum	E	Must be anodised electrolytically.
Titanium/Tantalum	950-1150	60	Vacuum	E	Must be anodised electrolytically.
Lead/Tin	100-150	60	N_2	E
Lead/Pewter	100-150	60	N_2	E
Aluminium	350-450	60	Ar	T	Use of different aluminium alloys produces anodising differential.

COMPATABILITY TABLE

The chart below is an indicator only; for more detailed information it is necessary to reference the specific properties of the metals to be used.

Easy to bond, good working characteristics

Easy to bond, difficult working characteristics

Difficult to bond, good working characteristics

Difficult to bond, difficult working characteristics

Incompatible to bond, deform or as a colour combination

Metals compatibility matrix with the following metals listed across the top and down the side: Gold, Platinum, Palladium, Fine Silver, Sterling Silver, Shibuishi, Shakudo, Copper, Gilding Metal, Brass, Bronze, Nickel, Nickel Silver, Monel Metal, Iron, Stainless Steel, Titanium, Niobium, Tantalum, Lead, Tin, Aluminium.

1. Fine silver/copper

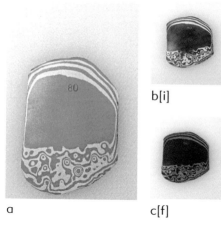

a

b[i]

c[f]

2. Fine silver/shibuishi/gilding metal

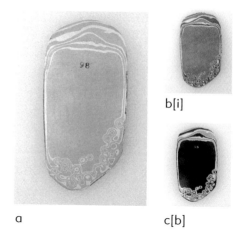

a

b[i]

c[b]

3. Fine silver/shakudo

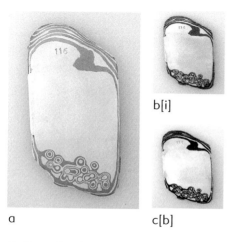

a

b[i]

c[b]

4. Fine silver/brass

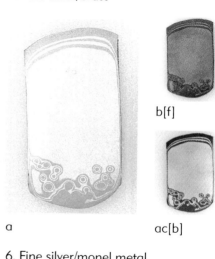

a

b[f]

ac[b]

5. Fine silver/nickel silver

a

b[e]

c[f]

6. Fine silver/monel metal

a

b[k]

c[g]

7. Fine silver/iron

a

b[h]

c[i]

8. Fine silver/stainless steel

a

b[g+l]

c[e]

9. Fine silver/titanium a

a

b[l]

c[h+l]

10. Shibuishi /copper

a

b[i]

c[b]

11. Shibuishi/shakudo

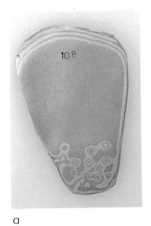

a

b[i]

c[b]

12. Shibuishi /bronze

a

b[i]

c[b]

13. Copper/gilding metal

a

b[i]

c[b]

14. Copper/brass

a

b[i]

c[g]

15. Copper/bronze

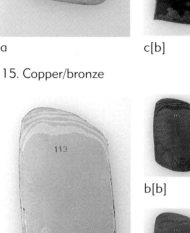

a

b[b]

c[f]

16. Copper/nickel silver

a

b[e]

c[g]

17. Coppe/monel metal

a

b[i]

c[k]

18. Copper/iron

a

b[i]

c[c]

111

19. Copper/stainless steel

a

b[i]

c[g]

20. Copper/titanium

a

b[i+l]

c[b+l]

21. Brass/bronze

a

b[g

c[b]

22. Brass/nickel silver

a

b[g]

c[b]

23. Brass/Monel metal

a

b[]

c[c]

24. Brass/iron

a

b[g]

c[i]

25. Brass/stainless steel

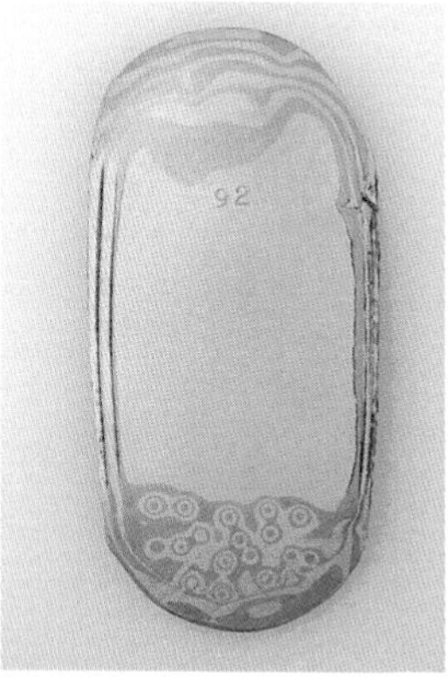

a

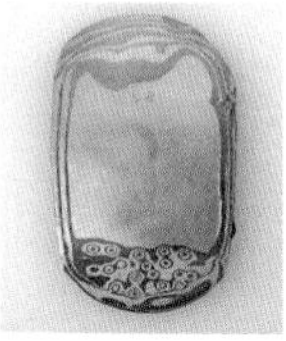

b[l]

c[g+l]

26. Bronze/nickel silver

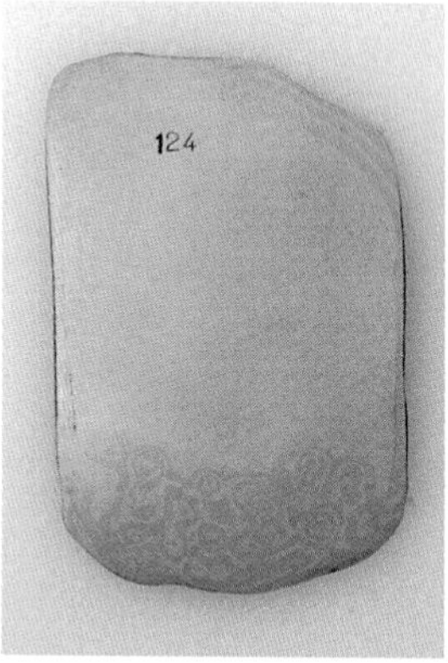

a

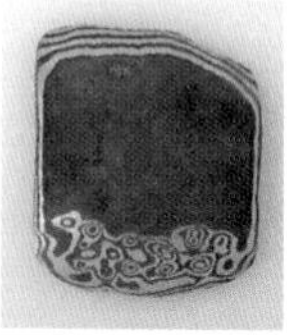

b[b]

c[i]

27. Nickel silver/iron

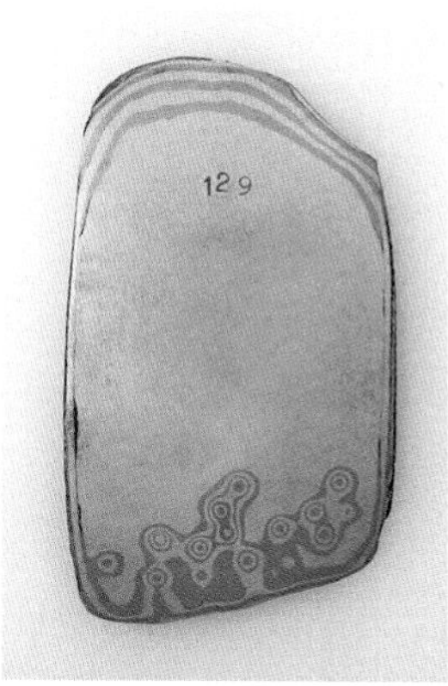

a

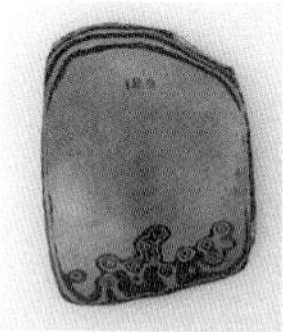

b[i]

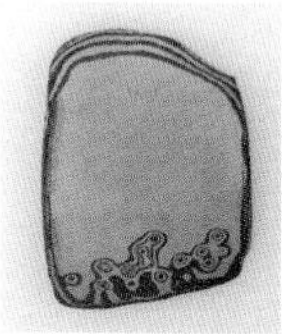

c[l]

28. Iron/stainless steel

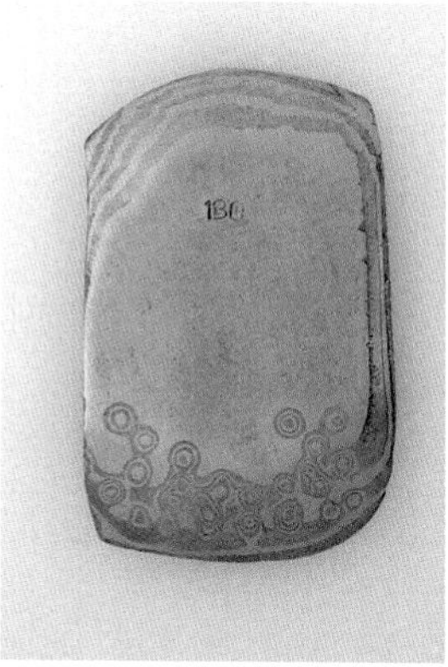

a

b[j]

c[j+l]

29. Aluminium alloys

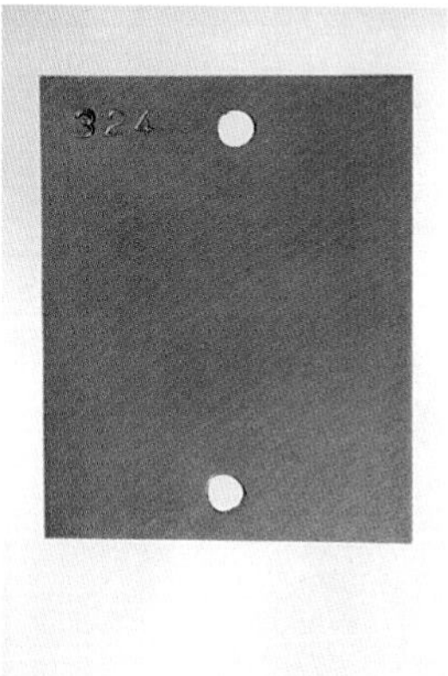

a[m]

b[m]

c[m]

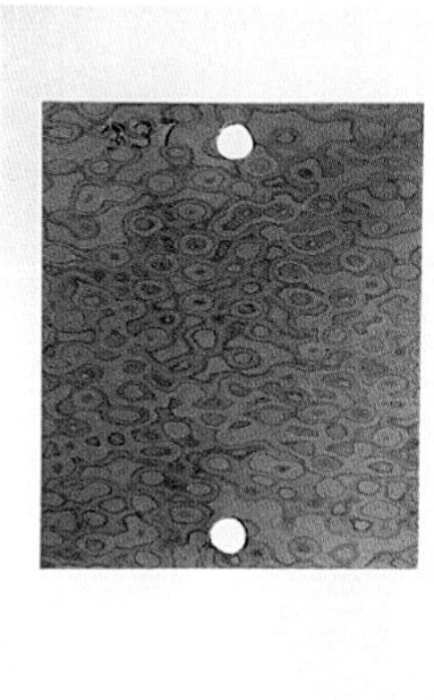

30. Aluminium/nickel

d[m]

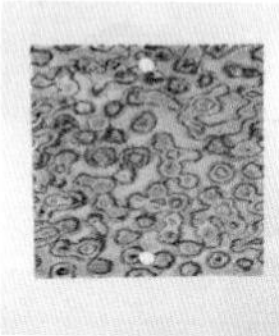

[m]

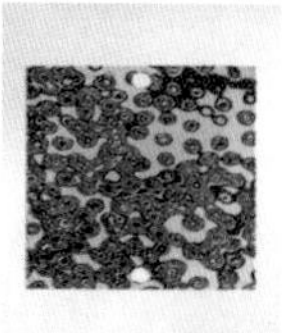

31. Aluminium/copper [b]

113

CHAPTER 14

Gallery

Plate 1. Pair of saké cups. Ø55cm x h40cm. 22ct. gold/ palladium alloy mokumé gane. Photo R. Muggleton

Since its invention, mokumé gane has been a process that requires considerable practical expertise in the production of the raw material, i.e. a billet of laminated metals. The application of modern metallurgical knowledge and practices lessens the problems associated with the making of a billet. The application of modern metallurgical knowledge also provides the potential to produce entirely new mokumé gane combinations. The problem shifts to the development of this potential and exploitation of the bonded metals – how to deform them, how to manipulate them, how to pattern them and how to use them creatively.

The images included in the following pages are a selection taken from 10 years of making objects out of mokumé gane. It can be seen that my work has evolved into simple vessel forms. Perhaps this is because of endless potential variations in metals, combinations, patterns and colours. I personally am obsessed with the vessel, particularly bowls and this presents a great challenge in that every new piece is a new experiment – each bowl is unique; indeed it seems possible to make bowls forever without repetition. Perhaps my interpretation is a little too simple, too conventional, and as such, it will be interesting to see what others can make of these new metals.

In the captions to the images, the suffixes in brackets at the end refers to:

First bracket-patterning technique.

Second bracket-colouring or patination technique.

Plate 2. *The Other Cup.* (a) Ø90cm x h35cm, 915 gold/silver/palladium alloy mokumé gane. (b) Ø85cm x h85cm, 925 Silver rim, aluminium mokumé gane. Photo R. Muggleton

Plate 4. Bowl. Ø140cm x h60cm. 925 silver rim, fine silver/shibuishi/copper mokumé gane.
Photo I. Haigh

Plate 3. Bowl. Ø105cm x h105cm, silver/copper mokumé gane.
Photo T. Bogue

Plate 6. Bowl. Ø195cm x h60cm. 925 silver rim, fine silver/nickel mokumé gane. Photo T. Bogue.

Plate 5. Beaker. Ø75cm x h100cm. 925 silver rim, fine silver/gilding metal mokumé gane. Photo I. Haigh

Plate 7. Wave form bowl. Ø170 cm x h45cm. 925 silver rim, fine silver/iron mokumé gane. Photo R. Muggleton

Plate 8. Bowl. Ø110cm x h75cm. 925 silver rim, shibuishi/copper mokumé gane. Makower Collection, Victoria & Albert Museum. Photo I. Haigh

Plate 9. Bowl. Ø120cm x h85cm. 925 silver rim, copper/gilding metal mokumé gane, gilded inside. Hamilton Regional Art Gallery. Photo T. Bogue

Plate 10. Bowl. Ø105cm x h65cm. 925 silver rim, copper/brass mokumé gane. Hamilton Regional Art Gallery. Photo T. Bogue

Plate 11. *Windows*, beaker, Ø85cm x h95cm. Copper/nickel mokumé gane, silver/nickel mokumé gane foot. Photo R. Muggleton

Plate 12. *The Burning Bowl.* Ø155cm x h65cm. 925 silver rim & foot, copper/iron mokumé gane. Photo R. Muggleton

Plate 13. *Flower Bowl.* Ø140cm x h85cm, copper/brass/gilding metal mokumé gane. Photo R. Muggleton

Plate 14. Bowl. Ø140cm x h35cm. 925 silver rim, copper/stainless steel mokumé gane. Makower Collection, Victoria & Albert Museum. Photo I. Haigh

Plate 15. Bowl. Ø155cm x h50cm. 925 silver rim, brass/iron mokumé gane, gilded outside. Photo T. Bogue

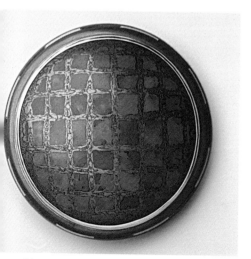

Plate 16. Shield brooch #4. 55Ø. 925 silver, copper, copper/titanium mokumé gane. Science Museum. Photo I. Ferguson

Plate 17. Bowl. Ø105cm x h90cm. Gilding metal/nickel mokumé gane. Photo T. Bogue

119

Plate 18. *Starry Night bowl.* Ø165cm x h100cm, copper rim, fine silver/shibuishi/gilding metal mokumé gane. Hamilton Regional Art Gallery. Photo R. Muggleton

Plate 19. *Summers Night Bowl.* 170Ø x 45h. 925 Silver rim, copper/titanium Mokumé Gane. Royal Museums of Scotland.

Plate 20. Aluminium bowl #7 - (Amaze-in Aluminium). Ø160cm x h70cm. 925 silver rim, aluminium mokumé gane. Photo R. Muggleton

Plate 21. Shield brooch #7. 55Ø. 925 silver, fine silver/gilding metal mokumé gane. Photo T. Bogue

Plate 22. *Maundy bowl.* Ø120cm x h45cm. 925 silver rim, copper/nickel silver mokumé gane. Science Museum. Photo I. Haigh

Plate 23. Vase. Ø125cm x h95cm. 925 silver rim and liner, aluminium mokumé gane. Photo R. Muggleton

Plate 24. Vase. Ø100cm x h110cm.
Silver/gilding metal mokumé gane.
Photo R. Muggleton

Plate 25. *Sea Foam vase.* Ø125cm x
h125cm. 925 silver rim and liner, silver/
nickel mokumé gane. Photo R. Muggleton

Plate 26. Aluminium bowl #5 - (Dislocation Bowl). Ø145cm x h55cm. 925 silver
rim, aluminium mokumé gane. Courtesy of the Science Museum.
Photo R. Muggleton

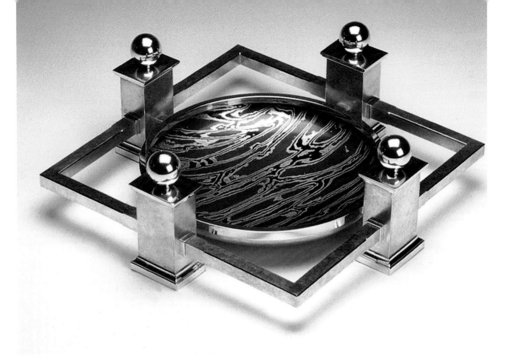

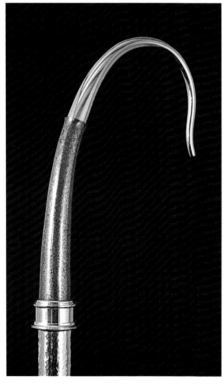

Plate 27. *Offering Bowl for a Barren Land.* Ø225cm x Ø225cm x h85cm. 925 silver, fine silver/copper/gilding metal mokumé gane.
Photo I. Haigh

Plate 29. Bowl. Ø105cm x h65cm. 925 silver rim, fine silver/gilding metal mokumé gane.
Photo T. Bogue

Note: All pieces by the author, unless otherwise stated.

Plate 28. *Crosier for an Archbishop.* (detail) Ø35-55cm x Ø200cm x h2050cm. 925 silver, copper/nickel mokumé gane. Sassafras.
Photo R. Muggleton

Bibliography

Ard, W., (ed.); 'Return to the Forge: Extended Research into mokumé-gane and Granulation', *Metalsmith Papers 1977-1980* – The Society of North American Goldsmiths, 1980.

Ard, W.; 'Studio Mokumé', *Metalsmith, Vol. 2, No. 2, Winter 1981*, pp. 46-51.

Audsley, G.A., *The Ornamental Arts of Japan*, Sampson Low, Marston, Searle & Rivington, London, 1882.

AWS Welding Handbook, 7th ed., Vol. 3, Resistance and solid state welding and other joining processes, American Welding Society, Miami, 1980.

Baldwin, P.; 'mokumé gane', *American Jewellery Manufacturer, Vol. 35 No. 4, April 1987*, pp. 22-8.

Barnes, R.S. and Masey D.J., 'The Effect of Pressure Upon Void Formation in Diffusion Couples', *Acta Metallurgica, Vol. 6, January 1958*, pp. 1-7.

Bradbury, F., *History of Old Sheffield Plate*, J. W. Northland Ltd, London, 1968.

Chang, Y.A., Neumann, J.P., Mikula, A., & Goldberg, D.; *Phase Diagrams and Thermodynamic Properties of Ternary Copper-Metal Systems*, International Copper Research Association Inc., USA, 1979.

Clarke, E.C., *The Rolling of Strip, Sheet and Plate*, Chapman and Hall Ltd, London, 1967.

Desaguliers, J.T., *Phil. Trans. of the Royal Society, Vol. 33*, 1724 p. 345.

Gowland, W.; 'Metals and Metal-Working in Old Japan', *The Japan Society Transactions and Proceedings Vol. XIII*, London, 1915, pp. 20-99.

Hansen, M., *Constitution of Binary Alloys*, McGraw-Hill Inc., New York, 1958.

Harris, V. and Ogasawara, N., *Swords of the Samurai*, British Museum Publications Ltd, 1990.

Hughes, R. and Rowe, M., *The Colouring, Bronzing and Patination of Metals*, Thames & Hudson, London 1991.

Joly, H.L., Tomita, K., *Japanese Art & Handicraft* (The 'Red Cross' Catalogue), Robert G. Sawers Publishing, London, 1976.

Kretchmer, S.D.; 'Layered Gold', *Aurum (English Ed.), No. 25, Spring 1986*, pp. 25-33.
Kurrein, M., *Plasticity of Metals*, Griffin, London, 1964.

Maryon, H., *Metalwork and Enamelling*, Dover, London, 1971.

Massalski, T. B. (ed.); *Binary Alloy Phase Diagrams*, American Society of Metals, 1986.

Midgett, S., *Mokumé Gane in the Small Shop*, Earthshine Press, North Carolina, 1994.

Midgett, S., *Mokumé Gane; A Comprehensive Study*, Earthshine Press, North Carolina 2000.

Morgan, M., Bronze mokumé-gane *Metalsmith, Vol. 4 No. 3 Spring 1983*

Pijanowski, G. and H.S., 'Laminations of Non-Ferrous Metals by Diffusion and Update: mokumé gane Wood Grain-Metal', *Metalsmith Papers 1977-1980* – The Society of North American Goldsmiths, Milwaukee, 1980.

Pijanowski, H.S. and G., 'Update II: Mokumé Gane', *Metalsmith, Vol. 4, No. 3, Spring 1983*, pp. 35, 36.

Pijanowski, H.S. and G., Workshop: mokumé-gane', *Craft Horizons, Vol. 38, No. 1, pp. 32-5.*

Roberts-Austen W.C., Cantor Lectures *Journal of the Society of Arts, Vol. 36, 1888*, pp. 1137-1146 and *Vol. 41, 1893*, pp. 1007-1043.

Roberts-Austen, W.C., Phil. *Trans. of the Royal Society, Vol. 187, 1896*, p. 383.

Roberts-Austen, W.C., *Proceedings*

of the Royal Society, Vol. 67, 1900, p. 101.

Ruoff, A.L., *Introduction to Materials Science* Prentice-Hall Inc., New Jersey 1972.

Schwartz, M.M., *Metal Joining Manual*, McGraw-Hill Inc., New York, 1983.

Smithells Metals Reference Book 6th ed., Butterworth & Co., London, 1983.

Stephenson D.J. (ed.), *Diffusion Bonding 2*, Elsevier Applied Science, London, 1991.

Taubman R., 'Update II: Mokumé-Gane Pattern Research', *Metalsmith, Vol. 4, No. 3, Spring, 1983* pp. 39-41.

Tylecote, R.F., *A History of Metallurgy*, The Metals Society, London, 1976.

Tylecote, R.F., *The Solid Phase Welding of Metals*, Edward Arnold (Publishers) Ltd, London, 1968.

Untracht, O., *Metal Techniques for Craftsmen*, Doubleday, New York, 1968.

Untracht, O., *Jewellery Concepts and Technology*, Robert Hale, London, 1982.

Vaidyanath, L.R., and Milner, D.R., 'Significance of Surface Preparation in Cold Pressure Welding', *British Welding Journal, Jan. 1960*, pp. 1-6.

Villiers, P., Prince, A., and Okamoto, H., *Handbook of Ternary Alloy Phase Diagrams*, ASM International Publishers, USA, 1995.

Von Neumann, R., *The Design and Creation of Jewelry*, 3rd ed., Chilton Book Company, Pennsylvania USA, 1982.

Wilson, H., *Silverwork and Jewellery*, Pitman Publishing Ltd, London, 1948.

Glossary

Asperities small ridges of metal left on a surface after abrasive milling or cleaning.

Billet block of unprocessed metal.

Binary consisting of two parts or constituents.

Blacksmiths forge a traditional metal heating procedure used worldwide, consisting of a forced air fed coal or coke fire in a brick hearth.

Bleed valve screw valve to allow the removal of a gas/liquid from a closed container or system.

Clamshell furnace a type of heating furnace that splits down the middle like a bi-valve.

Combination the metals combined in a mokumé billet.

Controlled atmosphere an enclosed atmosphere different to normal air.

Diffusion dispersal and movement of atoms through a substance; diffused.

Eutectic the lowest melting point of an alloy system, dependent on a particular proportion of the metals involved.

Fusion the melting of a substance and the joining of substances by melting; fused.

Guri layered black and red lacquer technique used in Japan.

Guri Bori early name for mokumé, due to its similarity to the abovementioned.

Intermetallic a chemical compound of two or more metals exhibiting particular properties, usually crystalline brittleness, e.g. Silicon Carbide and Titanium Cuprate.

Interstitial diffusion interstice, the space between atoms in a crystal lattice.

Jig device for controlling/containing a process or production.

Kirkendall porosity porosity in a metal caused by the excessively rapid diffusion of atoms to another position.

Kuromido Japanese alloy of 1% arsenic in copper.

Laminate a metal layer within a piece of mokumé.

pl. laminae.

Liquidus the temperature at which a metal becomes totally liquid.

Mokumé Gane. Japanese for eye of wood grain metal.

Muffle a container for a controlled atmosphere.

Patina protective layer applied to a metal surface using a chemical conversion process.

Phase diagram shows the thermal reactions of all the constituents in all their proportions in an alloy. Limited to binary and tertiary alloys.

Platen flat supporting plate, usually part of a jig/tool.

Quaternary consisting of four parts or constituents.

Repousseé raising a metal surface by punching/embossing from the back.

Rokusho Japanese patination chemical of undetermined composition; generally assumed to be a complex of copper salts including sulphates and acetates.

Roll-over the rounding of the edges of a sheet of metal caused by shear cutting.

Shakudo literally, red copper. Japanese alloy of 2 to 5% gold in copper.

Shibuishi literally, one fourth part. Japanese alloy of 25 to 50% silver in copper.

Soldering the joining of metal components using a lower melting point metal.

Solidus the temperature at which a metal becomes totally solid.

Substitutional diffusion where one atom moves to a vacancy, to be replaced by a substitute atom.

Tertiary consisting of three parts or constituents.

Torque plate system a jig for containing a billet of mokumé, using the torque applied to the bolts to apply pressure.

Traditional process/metal those processes and metals developed in Japan up until the end of the 19th century.

Tsuba removable guard to a Japanese sword blade.

Suppliers

The Sheffield College
Hillsborough LRC

UK

ABRASIVES

Blackson & Kenridge Ltd
Unit 12a, Fleetway West Business Park
Greenford
Middlesex UB6 7JU
Tel: 020 8991 578

Hermes Abrasives Ltd
Severalls Park
Wyncolls Rd
Colchester
Essex CO4 4LW
Tel: 01206 754400

CHEMICALS

Merck Ltd
Merck House
Seldown Lane
Poole
Dorset BH15 1TD
Tel: 01202 669700

Sigma-Aldrich Co. Ltd
The Old Brickyard
New Road
Gillingham
Dorset SP8 4XT
Tel: 01747 82211

FURNACES

Carbolite
Parsons Lane
Hope Valley
Derbys S33 6RE
Tel: 01433 620011

Lenton Thermal Designs Ltd
Parsons Lane

Hope Valley
Derbys S33 6RE
Tel: 01433 621515

Severn Furnaces Ltd
Unit 17-19 Walker Way Ind. Estate
Thornbury
Bristol, Avon BS35 3US
Tel: 01454 414600

INSULATORS

Tenmat Ltd
Asburton Road West
Trafford Park
Manchester M17 1RU
Tel: 061 872 2181

METALS

Aalco
Harrimans Lane
Lenton Lane Ind. Estate
Nottingham
Notts. NG7 2SD
Tel: 0115 988 2600
(*Non-Ferrous; copper, brass, etc.*)

Aalco
Unit 2, Slough Trading Estate
552 Fairlie Road
SLOUGH
Berks   SL1 4PY
Tel: 01753 619900
(*Aluminium*)

Aalco
Unit F, Forgeway Brown
Lees Road Ind. Estate, Knypersley
Staffs. ST8 7DN
Tel: 01782 375700
(*Stainless*)

Amari Metals International
Upper Brook Street
Walsall
West Midl. WS2 9PD
Tel: 01922 636141
(*Monel, Nickel, Titanium*)

Cookson Precious Metals Ltd
Theba House
49 - 50 Hatton Gardens
London EC1N 8YS
Tel: 020 7400 6500
(*Precious metals*)

Fays Metals Ltd
Unit 4
37 Colville Road
London W3 8BL
Tel: 0208 993 8883
(*Non-Ferrous; copper, brass, etc.*)

Goodfellows
Cambridge Science Park
Milton Road
Cambridge CB4 4DJ
Tel: 0223 568068
Fax: 0223 420639
(*Pure Metals - all kinds*)

Metalor Ltd
104 - 105 Saffron Hill
London EC1N 8HB
Tel: 0207 405 5298
(*Precious metals*)

Smiths Metal Centres Ltd
42-56 Tottenham Rd
London N1 4BZ
Tel: 0207 241 2430

Thesco Ltd Royds Mills
Windsor Street
Sheffield S4 7W
(*Germanium Silver*)
Tel: 0114 272 0966
Fax: 0114 275 2655

NIMONIC FITTINGS

Incotest Ltd
Wiggin Works
Holmer Road, Hereford
Herts HR4 9SL
Tel: 01432 352230

PAPER TOWELS

Kimberley Clark (Europe)
35 London Road
Reigate
Surrey RH2 9PZ
Tel: 01737 736000

Georgia-Pacific GB Ltd
Pembroke House, Pembroke Rd
Ruislip
Middlesex HA4 8NQ
Tel: 01895 626500

PRESSES

Power Team (UK) Ltd
(also called LES)
Unit 43, IMEX Business Park
Birmingham
West Midlands B11 2AL
Tel: 01207 507077

USA

James E. Binnan
Bellingham
WA
Tel: +360 756 6550
Fax: +360 756 2160

Steve Midgett
Earthshine Mokumé Inc
447 Louisa Chapel Road
Franklin
NC 28734
Tel: +1(800) 374 6423
Fax: +1(800) 349 4924

Index